ALL THE PAINTINGS OF
LORENZO LOTTO
Part I
VOLUME SIXTEEN
in the
Complete Library of World Art

The Complete Library of World Art

ALL THE PAINTINGS

OF **LORENZO LOTTO**

Part I

By PIERO BIANCONI

Translated from the Italian by

PAUL COLACICCHI

HAWTHORN BOOKS, INC.

Publishers · New York

Manufactured in Great Britain by Jarrold & Sons Ltd, Norwich

CONTENTS

LORENZO LOTTO

Life and Work

LORENZO LOTTO was about twenty-five years old when he received the highest praise of his whole career: a document of 1505 proclaimed him *pictor celeberrimus* (most outstanding painter). This happened when Lotto, a Venetian, was living at Treviso, a provincial town that he adopted as his home for a time. During his life he worked for long periods in the countryside around Treviso, Ancona and Bergamo, never staying long in Venice where he must have found little recognition among the affluent official classes. Even in the provinces he attracted meager praise, perhaps because of his nomadic habits which increased as he grew older.

The world took little notice of Lotto while he was alive, and after his death his work commanded casual attention among art critics. For centuries he was half-forgotten, but towards the end of the nineteenth century, a new awareness of his paintings emerged, followed by an eager reassessment of their artistic value. The reasons for this belated appreciation were partly to be found in the unusually modern even "restless" quality of his spirit and in his anguished sensitivity, for Lotto belongs to that magnificent family of high-strung artists whom Marcel Proust considered the salt of the earth. The reappraisal was also partly due to the artist's strikingly original pictorial language, so prophetic of much that was to come.

At the end of the nineteenth century, while local biographers were busily attempting to throw light on the course

7

of Lotto's life, Bernard Berenson traced the artist's career and published an essay, rich with psychological insight into Lotto's complex personality, that still is considered fundamental. Berenson's text has remained practically unaltered and is now in its third edition. At about the same time as Berenson's essay was published, Lotto's "Book of Accounts" was discovered. It contributed—perhaps too effectively—to a reconstruction of the artist's life at a time when he was nearing old age (he began entering his accounts in the book in 1538 when he was fifty-eight years old). The image we have of Lotto as an old man therefore tends to color the whole of his work, accenting its restless, feverish character.

The man is rarely so evident in his art as is Lotto, sometimes so excessively that it fails. For this reason one is easily tempted to think of Lotto's life and work in a modern, romantic key and to consider him almost a *peintre maudit* before his time.

On the other hand, Lotto has been called an important forerunner. After Berenson, one should mention among the critics who have shown a particular interest in him, Robert Longhi, who pointed out in Lotto one of the strong sensibilities lying behind Caravaggio: a sense, that is, for the modest and poetic reality that surrounds naturally lighted objects. Longhi's research probed peripheral areas outside the central, more representational Renaissance tradition. New attention was being given to artists who had hitherto been marginal, misunderstood or forgotten—romantic, wandering figures like Lotto, Amico Aspertini and others whom Longhi describes as "mingling in the crowds that appear at dusk to inscribe their names among the ruins, grottoes, and catacombs."

This new interest, whether intent on psychological or romantic interpretations, or bent on altering the traditional history of painting, has contributed to the increasing authority of Lotto's name. The great Venice Exhibition of 1953 should be regarded as a result of the need for general consideration of this fascinating artist. It rewarded the long, painstaking process of study and reappraisal.

But the Exhibition failed to amplify what we know of Lotto's formative years; in fact, Venice proved to be a hard test for some works, cutting down the number previously attributed to Lotto. He was born in 1480 and, although his artistic education undoubtedly took place in Venice, his pictorial language from the very beginning showed a definite character, linked though it may have been to that of Alvise Vivarini (according to Berenson who, however, in his third edition modifies this influence), of the Muranese School, of Diana and Pennacchi (Banti), of Antonello da Messina, Giovanni Bellini and Jacopo de'Barbari. The last-named probably made Lotto aware of the Northern masters who were to contribute so much to his technique. Then there are the cultural influences of such centers as the Fondaco dei Tedeschi, and the impression made by Dürer during his second stay in Venice. We should remember the *Madonna of the Rosary* (now at Prague) which Dürer painted for the Church of San Bartolomeo, and his *Christ Among the Elders* (1506; Thyssen Collection, Lugano), some obvious elements of which can be discerned in Lotto's works. In the midst of all these possibly disruptive influences, Lotto still succeeded in developing his own personality, and perhaps Leonello Venturi was right in describing him as a self-taught artist. Lotto, moreover, for all of his helpers and apprentices, never had a student worthy of being his successor.

The critic Coletti is an ardent supporter of the theory that Lotto's education owed much to the artists of the Marches, where he must have studied Melozzo da Forli and Luca

Signorelli of Loreto; this theory is based on records of his early activities in this region. Among the formative lessons taught him by these artists, one should not overlook those Lotto might have gleaned from his predecessor Crivelli, whose spirit had so many affinities to his own. This is particularly true if one examines such early works as the great *Recanati Polyptych* of 1508, in which the jewelry and embroidery work on the vestments are strongly reminiscent of Crivelli, or the craftsmanlike fineness of the details which Lotto, however, brought up to the level of expressiveness found in modern still life.

If Lotto's first indisputable work, the *Madonna and Child with Saints* at Naples (1503; plate 1), reflects Bellini's manner, then *A Maiden's Dream* (plate 5) and the beautiful *St Jerome in the Wilderness* (1506; plate 11) reveal Lotto's own lyrical feeling for nature as seen through the eyes of the lonely traveler; the *St Jerome*, in fact, providing the first hints of a theme that will endure throughout his art. In his early portraits—*Bishop Bernardo de' Rossi* (1505; plate 3); the *Bust of a Woman* (plate 6); the cold *Bust of a Youth Against a White Curtain* (plate 16); and the pink and white *Bust of a Dominican Monk* (plate 18)—Lotto complicated his original rigid manner (so much like Antonello's) by adhering more closely yet imaginatively to reality and by giving his figures a gemlike coloring far removed from Giorgione's tonalities. But in these figures we still cannot find the passionate warmth and sense of participation that are characteristic of his mature portraiture. Even in the *Santa Cristina Altarpiece* the echoes of Antonello's *San Cassiano Altarpiece* are plain, just as Giorgione's presence is clear in Lotto's archaizing and polemical attitude. He renders homage to his masters, but with an uncertain sensitivity that tries to break up the architectonic firmness with shimmering light and softer coloring.

The artist's devotion to the Quattrocento masters renews itself in the archaic *Recanati Polyptych* (1508; plates 19–25). On the other hand, some admirable intuitions and innovations here again express Lotto's very personal resources; observe in the side wings the half-length figures of Saints (plate 24), at once fearful and ardent, or, in the *Pietà* (plate 21), how the ancient theme is rephrased with substantial pathos. In the central panel (plate 19), the bands of light cast from below help to break up the conventional symmetry of the composition; a new movement bends the forms to the point where their torment is felt and unmistakable. The same torment, contorting faces and forms, is again enacted in the *Madonna and Child with Saints* in Rome's Borghese Gallery (plate 17), painted in the same year—again the symmetry of the picture is broken up by light that beats fully on the Bishop and leaves St Onophrius in shadow, a device which Lotto obviously learned from Dürer.

Lotto's stay in Rome is proved by two payments made to him in 1509 and by evidence in his later works; there are, however, no documents relating to the length of his stay or to his activities there. Raphael, Bramantino, and Sodoma were then busily decorating the Vatican *Stanze*. The lack of information relating to Lotto, together with Raphael's overshadowing reputation, have long prevented any objective study of the relationship between the two masters, especially of the question of Lotto's possible influence on Raphael. A. Banti suggests that the two artists first met at Urbino in 1507, after which Lotto might have been summoned to Rome. Zampetti believes he may have painted the portraits of the Prelates in the *Mass of Bolsena* and Longhi goes so far as to identify Lotto's contributions to the *Stanze* landscapes and characters and to identify the artist himself in the figure of Aeschines in the *School of Athens*. So the gap in our knowledge of Lotto's life during the years between his stay at Recanati (1508) and his stay at Jesi (1512) is gradually being filled.

Michelangelo, who was then working in the Sistine Chapel, and even the Roman examples of classic antiquity had little or no effect on Lotto. Sodoma might have influenced his work with a touch of Leonardo's *sfumato*, thus preparing Lotto for his later use of Lombardesque light, but Lotto's chief contacts were probably with Bramantino, whom he was to meet again a few years later in Milan. A certain continuing preference for plain, enclosed architectural backgrounds even in a later work, *The Presentation in the Temple* at Loreto (plate 206), can be attributed to Bramantino's influence. One might imagine these two northern Italians walking and discoursing in the streets of Rome, one quiet and studious, the other brilliant and capricious; they were diverse but compatible, for both were alien to formal classicism. What other contacts Lotto may have had during these unexplored years is hard to say. Coletti suggests that the artist visited Florence where he may have come into contact with early Tuscan Mannerism in the small cloister of the Church of the Annunziata. We would willingly believe, though, that he had visited Lucca and had seen Aspertini's frescoes, with a spirit and emotion so similar to his own, in the Church of San Frediano.

But whatever Lotto did in Rome, and whoever inspired him there, it was Raphael's influence that finally freed him from the confines of the Quattrocento. Raphael is present to a troubling degree in the Jesi *Deposition* (1512; plate 28), the first work executed after the artist's stay in Rome. This composition is made up of figures caught in banal gestures which impair the artist's expression at a very critical moment in his development. But the clear quality of the landscape shows how some of Raphael's virtues might well have suited Lotto. The Recanati *Transfiguration* (plate 29), however, declines into coarseness with a curious rolling rhythm in its movement. Being near Raphael at first produced a temporary loss of direction in Lotto, but at the same time Lotto's colors became more fluid and transparent. The Roman experience was thus fundamentally important to Lotto's development.

Once in touch with Lombardesque naturalism—about 1512-13—Lotto's pictorial language became purer and more defined. In a more congenial world, he was able to find himself again and to absorb Da Vinci's lessons (particularly noticeable in the Dresden *Madonna and Child* of 1518; plate 48). To Roman classicism Lotto could now oppose a new wave of Northern influences, such as those perhaps of Altdorfer and Grünewald, though once again we cannot be sure.

In Lotto's first great work executed at Bergamo—where he stayed intermittently until 1526—*The Santo Stefano Altarpiece* (1516; plates 36-43)—we may observe this curious and restless artist recapitulating his experiences. With the exception of the influences already mentioned, and of a certain imitation of Titian, Lotto absorbed his lessons well, without suppressing his own perceptive powers. There may well be a trace of eclecticism in the cumbersome *Altarpiece*, solidly Bramantesque in its architectural scheme but airily capricious in its upper section (one is here reminded of Mantegna and the Ferrarese School). This is also true of the bizarre throne, but the tender play of light and shadow around the nude figure of St Sebastian, the more than merely plausible insight with which each character is painted, have an unmistakable accent of their own. This altarpiece may be considered as incorporating a series of experiments and as the final proof of a successful apprenticeship. This work was executed simultaneously with Correggio's *San Francesco Altarpiece*, and bears some singular parallels. There are indeed some odd similarities between the two artists, though one could not assume that they ever knew one another.

The Santo Stefano Altarpiece is now dismantled and we do not have a clear idea of the whole structure. However, from the three admirable panels of the predella (plates 38–40) we can easily discern how quickly Lotto's language matured in the course of their execution. We need only compare, to see this maturity, *The Deposition* (plate 39), so dramatically tense and vibrant, with the Jesi *Deposition* (plate 28), or else look closely at the elegant and energetic *Martyrdom of St Stephen* (plate 38), magnificent down to the last detail of its landscape.

Thus began the Bergamo cycle, that is to say, the fruits of Lotto's completed growth as an artist. When he was about forty years old, Lotto created the magnificent altarpieces of *San Bernardino* and *Santo Spirito* in Bergamo (1521; plates 50 and 54) in which his spirit unfolds more fully. In the former especially, there is new inventiveness—though Raphael's influence has not yet disappeared—in the light playing over the canopy, in the responsive eloquence of the Virgin poised, as she is, between light and shade, in the solemn gathering of old men below, in the flying Angels supporting the green canopy (plate 51), and in the unforgettable Angel crouching by the pedestal taking down the Virgin's words: he is all gold and rust colored; his small dark eyes appear to float in a face flattened by light (plate 52).

In the second altarpiece which, as Berenson notes, "has neither the freshness nor the depth of feeling" of the first, one is struck by the host of Angels "flying, dancing and making music." They have a fresh chromatic freedom and precede Correggio's daring *Cupola* in the Duomo at Parma by at least five years. Equally beautiful in opulent color and graceful rhythms are *The Marriage of St Catherine* (plate 64), one of Lotto's favorite subjects, and the *Portrait of Lucina Brembate* (plate 53).

In the portraits of this Bergamo period, Lotto was not yet passionately given to exploring and revealing intimate character, as he was to do later: his complacent and superficial Lucina, or Bonghi in *The Marriage of St Catherine* (plate 65) or *Messer Marsilio and His Bride* (plate 69) in the Prado, or again, the men and women of the Suardi family who watch in *St Clare Taking Her Vows* at Trescore (plates 80–81), all belong to a more placid breed than the one which interested Lotto in his late years. But in this Bergamo phase his painting was stronger, with none of the hesitations and faults which were to appear as he grew older. Were we ignorant of his later failings and capitulations, were we to know only his Bergamo period, and if that pathetic, heartbreaking "Book of Accounts" had never come to light, filled with petty revelations, humiliations, faulty contracts and accounts settled at a loss, our opinion of Lorenzo Lotto would be very different. He would appear a tranquil, satisfied man, his art assured, deliberate, and conscious of its worth. How removed is Lotto of the Bergamo period from the old man living on the charity of his friends and relatives, often grateful for a bowl of soup from some convent. Bergamo echoes with the sound of laughter, of practical jokes and cordiality. We can point out the humor of the newlyweds (plate 69) or the arch puzzle of the *Portrait of Lucina Brembate* (plate 53).

In the same period, however, other forces were manifest in Lotto's development: the anguished pathos of *The Deposition* (plate 47; now practically ruined); the drama of *Christ*

Taking Leave of His Mother (1521; plate 56), a sacred representation leaning towards the compunction of the Counter-Reformation, a direction Lotto was to take more and more. There was also a more amiable tendency, a narrative vein displayed in delicate small works such as *Susannah and the Elders* (1517; plate 45), recounted in the mode of Flemish miniatures with its waving scrolls and exaggerated postures; in the *Legends of SS Barbara, Clare, and Mary Magdalen* in the Suardi Chapel at Trescore (1524; plates 73–87 and folded reproduction). Here, the luminosity of a watercolor lights the golden crops, green foliage and fields, forming the setting for some delightful architecture; the narrative unfolds with unashamed gusto and each episode is depicted in an atmosphere of candor; even the atrocities inflicted on Barbara have the gentle, disarming tone of a fairytale told to children. This seems so incredible in an Italy where Raphael had been dead only four years. One is strongly tempted to think again of some Northern stimuli, remembering especially the beautiful *Intarsias* of the choir stalls in the Church of Santa Maria Maggiore at Bergamo (plates 88–93), a superb example of Lotto's inventiveness.

In or about 1526, the artist went back to Venice, or rather, chose that city as the center of his nomadic life between Treviso and the Marches, particularly the towns of Recanati, Jesi and Ancona. During the years following the Bergamo period (from about 1526 to 1532), his artistic capabilities were fulfilled and his work attains a clear articulation. But in those same years his composure appears to have been disturbed by subconscious tremors, a forewarning, perhaps, of a shadowed future that augments and deepens his lyricism.

In 1526, Lotto executed the Jesi panel depicting the *Madonna Enthroned with Saints* (plate 107b). The cardinal-red of Jerome's robe is bold against the green curtain (many of Lotto's curtains are green and billowing); the bald St Joseph, dressed as a pilgrim, kneels by a blossoming rose bush. Then come other great paintings: *The Adoration of the Shepherds* at Brescia (plate 129), conceived as a sacred representation celebrating Christmas, with pale, melancholy donors in the role of shepherds. Here a new color scheme produces a balance of whites, blacks, browns, and yellows; the Virgin is wrapped in the soft opulence of a deep blue robe and St Joseph, in red, stands out against the shadow just under the lighted window; the donkey's ears, silhouetted in the open door, repeat the spread of the Angel's wings behind Joseph. A tender family atmosphere of the Northern type, perfect balance, and supreme control of the medium are all evident in this picture; the innovations presage Savoldo and Caravaggio. The *Sacra Conversazione* at Vienna (plate 131) may have been executed in the same period: the Virgin in a light porcelain-blue robe sits under a spreading tree with an Angel holding a wreath of blossoms over her head. The Venetian theme is re-created here with great lyrical feeling. Not too far in time from these two works must be the Recanati *Annunciation* (plate 132). It should be seen in its own setting, the small Oratory of the Church of Santa Maria sopra Mercanti, all green and gold, to appreciate the sudden disruption brought into the quiet room by the Angel's arrival and the contrast between the messenger with his impetuosity and cold coloring and the Virgin dressed in red and violet-pink, staring in unbelieving terror.

These works represent the summit of Lotto's new and most complete form of lyricism, and to them one should perhaps add the landscape in *St Nicholas of Bari in Glory* in the Church of the Carmini at Venice (plates 133–34) in

which the artist's poetic feeling triumphs over the somewhat lifeless conformity, Titian-like, of the figures in the
heavens. For, in contrast, the landscape crawls with movement—animals, their drivers, and numerous active figures.
We can measure Lotto's progress on his lonely road by com-
paring this painting with the detailed and rigid *St Jerome in
the Wilderness* in the Louvre (plate 10), executed twenty-three
years earlier.

The Assumption of the Virgin at Celana (1527; plate 115) is
so bold in its whipping lines and curves, in the exuberant
spectacle, that one suspects Lotto worked at times with an
eye on his painting's destination and the fee he had been
promised. But this irreverent doubt is promptly dispelled by
the superb Archangel Gabriel in *The Ponteranica Polyptych*
(plate 118) executed practically at the same time as *The
Assumption*. The great *Crucifixion* at Monte San Giusto (1531;
plate 148) is one of Lotto's overwhelming successes. Its
drama would be confusing were it not for the strong frame
of light which helps to establish the planes in their proper
order. The whole composition is marked by a tremendous
narrative force which, beneath the crucifixes livid in the dark
of night, is so violent that it strains the perspective. The
three-dimensional effect and the lurid, expressive colors give
the canvas a visionary, hallucinated appearance.

About this time another instance occurred of the artist's
disconcerting ability to change mood and palette: in the Jesi
Visitation (plate 145b), painted with layer upon layer of cold
colors, we see the heavy human pathos of the pregnant old
woman and the solidity of the still life on the mantelpiece,
reminiscent of the mantel in the Recanati *Annunciation* (plate
132). Then Lotto changes again: after the gloomy *Visitation*
he executed (also at Jesi) the bright yellow and red *St
Lucy Altarpiece* (1532; plate 154). This, however, is totally

surpassed by its predella (plates 156–58), one of the artist's greatest achievements. In the lively little scenes of the predella, the architectural elements, the banners, the shouting crowds are all steeped in a kind of dusty light that one is forced to describe as Impressionistic. The chromatic intensity, the vibrating clearness, the calculated movement of this predella give to Lotto's art a modern quality even more surprising when one remembers that he was then fifty years old. Only eight years before he had painted the Trescore frescoes. Another look at their graceful, miniature-like finish will be enough to perceive the nature of Lotto's lonely progression.

At this time, Lotto's portraits: *A Dominican Steward* (1526; plate 111), *Andrea Odoni* (1527; plate 123), *Gentleman Holding a Golden Claw* (plate 125), and probably the *Young Man in His Study* (plate 126) seem to acquire a more subtle but vibrant sense of life and reveal a *rapport* between artist and subject as well as a closer study. The artist's nature, as expressed through his portraits, appears more likable, affectionate rather than imperious; his pictorial language sustains a greater range of emotions. His forms are increasingly active, and broken up by a fine network of light, the surface movement symbolizing perhaps the transient nature of all things. Lotto rejected the static form, intellectually contemplated— and this was what saved him from the influence of the Tuscan artists. His undetermined space, and the occasional indifference to perspective (as rightly observed by Coletti), yields a stronger impression of the fleeting moment. Lotto was passionately concerned with feelings, and they are forever crowding him. He lacks, as Berenson has shrewdly noted, the detachment with which the great have expressed their epochs, an impersonal attitude that is, perhaps, the leaven of genius.

This explains why Lotto, an artist deeply and wholly

committed to sentiment, was excluded from that rational and formal spirit that is the substance of the Renaissance. He was impressed by the artists north of the Alps who stimulated his inherent taste for whims and caprices of form, which are denied those whose taste is for the normative and reasonable. We can well understand why Lotto, the individualist, felt the need to escape to the provinces where he might freely indulge in caprice and innovations, away from the overwhelming pictorial conventions of Venice, from the raised eyebrows of the *literati*, and the critical weight of the Titian School (in this context see Dolce's criticism of the altarpiece in the Church of the Carmini, plate 133, and Aretino's poisonous letter in the "Selected Criticism"). One cannot help but conclude that Lotto deliberately chose to live quietly and avoid renown. His commissions may have been more modest, coming as they did from communities of artisans and friars who probably haggled over prices and delivery dates, over the quality of his canvases and colors, but they at least granted him complete freedom of expression.

After 1532, at the end of his finest period, one is struck by the increasing frequency of irregular tonalities and other failings in Lotto's works. At times it would seem as if anxiety and impatience prevented his carrying through his conceptions with certainty. Nevertheless, his masterpieces—for there were more to come—are perhaps even more moving because of this very instability. The colors of the great *Madonna of the Rosary* at Cingoli (1539; plate 169) revert to gray tones, as they were to do in the *Madonna Enthroned with Four Saints*, the altarpiece in the Church of Santa Maria della Piazza at Ancona (plate 174), painted shortly afterwards. But over the lively composition of Saints gathered around the

Virgin blooms a mystical tree, and from its branches hang fifteen roundels, each containing a Mystery of the Rosary (plates 171–73). These are so modern in execution that some critics, among them Cavalcaselle, suspected them to be eighteenth-century additions.

The scenes are so freely conceived, the stories unfold so coherently, that one is reminded of the narrative genius first displayed by the Lotto of the Bergamo *Intarsias* and of the Trescore frescoes. One is also reminded of *The Intarsias* in the similarity of the twining Christ and the mystical tree to devotional prints, revealing a taste for popular art that Lotto never quite managed to discard. The pictorial treatment of the *tondi* is reminiscent of the Jesi *Visitation* (plate 145b) in its tone, in the lack of high coloring and in their religious piety. The many references to Lotto's support of the Reformation are very plausible, in the sense that his religious feeling was genuine, ardent and never satisfied.

Some of Lotto's compositions are pervaded by an extreme, mystical piety. A case in point is the Florence *Christ on the Cross* with its long, pietistic inscription on the reverse (see comment on plate 147), or *Christ Taking Leave of His Mother* (plate 56) which, like other works by Lotto, contains the agonized drama that was to become typical of the Counter-Reformation, revealing another relationship between Lotto and Correggio. It suggests, furthermore, "the composition of place" as advocated in his *Spiritual Exercises* by Ignatius of Loyola; that is, the meditative act of seeing the place in the mind and participating fully in its sacred drama. Lotto may have heard St Ignatius's sermons in Venice, for they were both there in 1536. We should add that Venice was the most important center in Italy of reform elements who were seeking true spirituality, but Lotto's activity there does not suggest that he embraced any heresy.

21

An increasing introspection and pictorial austerity become evident mainly in Lotto's portraits. They are, after all, the most interesting aspects of his work, for he was a formidable interrogator of souls, and constantly sought communication with an eagerness that seems to be shared by his sitters as he portrayed them.

The differences between Lotto and Titian have often been stressed: how Titian painted humanity with arrogant assurance, while Lotto painted what he saw, to an extent where often the mediocrity or indifference of his sitter affected the quality of the portrait. It is noticeable, for instance, that Lotto paid less attention to his female sitters (with the remarkable exception of the *Portrait of a Lady as Lucretia*, plate 136). But when artist and model were compatible, unforgettable masterpieces were born, such as the Gussoni family in the Brescia *Adoration of the Shepherds* (plates 129–130), the *Young Man in His Study* at Venice (plates 126–128), the *Man Aged Thirty-Seven* at Rome (plate 166) and the portraits of the *Old Man* and the *Elderly Gentleman* at Milan (plates 184 and 186). A whole gallery of weary people, ridden with fears and problems, seem to be denouncing life, its false pleasures and its vanity; the dying roses, the violets, the jasmine and the small skulls that everywhere appear in these paintings symbolize the pathetic sentiment of that era. They bring to mind Tasso and even Pascal.

We should not omit, among Lotto's great portraits, the *St Antoninus Altarpiece* (plates 175–78). In this canvas, two priests are depicted receiving petitions and giving money to the poor. They and the recipients strikingly express the artist's own charitable nature. The artist must have given much thought to the figures, especially the veiled women seen in profile near the center of the parapet (plate 178).

Lotto's imagination as well as his gentleness are embodied

in the flowers that appear constantly, both as symbols and as things of nature. As for animals, one could indeed devote a whole essay to Lotto's zoology: the frightened cat arching its back between the Virgin and the Angel in the Recanati *Annunciation* (plate 132); the little dog playing with the folds of a lady's skirt, the black cat lurking behind the pillars on the right, the rabbits watching the scene from the Italianate garden in *Christ Taking Leave of His Mother* in Berlin (plates 56–58); the green lizard on the desk of the *Young Man in His Study* at Venice (plate 127)—along with a scorpion, another lizard in the *St Jerome* at Madrid (plate 190); the ermine creeping over Chastity's bosom in *The Allegory of Chastity* in Rome (plate 138); the squirrel between Jesus and St Catherine in the *Madonna and Child with Saints* at Costa di Mezzate (plate 61); the little dogs at play in *The St Lucy Altarpiece* at Jesi (plate 156); and the dog tirelessly following St Barbara through all the scenes of her martyrdom in the great fresco at Trescore (plates 73–79).

Lotto's "Book of Accounts" records his life from 1538, when he was fifty-eight, to 1556, the year of his death, but as we have observed, it tends somewhat to distort the image of the artist, for it presents him as a vacillating, senile figure. No doubt he was an introvert, unstable, sensitive, and moody, now filled with ardor, now filled with depression and frustration: not, in any case, amenable. All these aspects became more marked in his old age. He changed his residence more and more often, moving from squalid lodgings in Venice, where he was badly cared for by sleazy old women, to the homes of relatives and friends: in 1540 he went to stay with his nephew, Mario d'Armano, at Venice; two years later he was at Treviso in the house of his friend, Ioan del Saon. Here the artist found his food was begrudgingly given, the lodging uncomfortable; he was surrounded by suspicion and gossip and could not find either the peace or the affection he craved, no matter, it seems, for all the doughnuts he brought home for the children, and the presents of rings, silk robes, golden shoes, and ivory combs he gave to the woman of the household. His interest, we may add incidentally, in feminine adornment is reflected in his art (see the casket on Venus' shoulder in *The Allegory of Chastity*, plate 137, and other details of jewelry and clothing throughout his work).

Lotto has been described as frigid because his female nudes are few and devoid of great warmth; in fact, payments "for undressing a woman naked" seldom appear in the "Book of Accounts." However, there is a greater and more significant warmth in other scenes, such as the mystical *Marriage of St Catherine*, for which the donor's request cannot have been entirely responsible, or in the several paintings of *St Sebastian* (plates 152–153), or in other ambiguous works such as the beautiful *Young Man* (possibly a *Young Woman*, plate 110). Undoubtedly Lotto controlled and even repressed his emotions by constant work, austere living and the study of bitter texts. He believed that "by spiritual meditation one rises above earthly things." In his will of 1546, the name of a woman catches our attention. It is Lucia Cadorina, the mother of a ten-year-old boy, a "washerwoman from San Moyse" to whom Lotto leaves ten ducats for having been "faithful to me in the Charity of Christ."

He was undoubtedly an educated man. This we know from his statements and from the garrulous "Book of Accounts" where he mentions reading the *Meditations* by Marcus Aurelius and the *De contemptu mundi*. During his unsuccessful attempt at leading a normal family life in the home of Ioan del Saon at Treviso, he tried to teach the children to read the Book of Psalms and to understand the work of Donatello.

His later years were tormented by a desire for peace which became stronger as his nature grew harsher. He longed for a family's love, or at least for the security of conventual life. In 1542, he asked to be buried "clad in religious garments," that is to say, in a monk's habit, and it was not by chance that he ended his days in a cloister at Loreto. In the "Book of Accounts" the theme of tranquillity recurs persistently. When he left Venice for Treviso, he explained that he was parting from his nephew "because of the many unsettling worries in that home," and that he was accepting Saon's hospitality because he was "advanced in years, bereft of a faithful housekeeper and very uneasy in mind." When he finally resolved to enter the cloister, he wrote of "appeasing life."

The old artist, in his search for peace, was harried by constant financial worry. He was continuously pawning his beloved jewels and engraved stones, or trying to sell some small canvases which he would send to Rome, Sicily, and Loreto. On leaving Venice in 1549, he entrusted a few cameos and jewels to his friend Sansovino who returned them to him a short while later. In 1550, when he settled in Ancona, he organized a public lottery of thirty of his works. "In the name of God, I have sent my paintings to a lottery," he wrote. His hopes were high but the result was disastrous.

His standing as an artist declined to that of the humblest craftsman: he undertook to paint numbers on hospital beds and angel wings for a *paolo* and a half apiece (a *paolo* was an old Papal coin of small denomination); heads of Madonnas on candles; procession standards and trumpets for village feasts. But even before this, the accounts include a fair number of minor undertakings, such as restoring old paintings and Flemish miniatures, completing pictures begun by other artists, and decorating wooden statues. Perhaps he needed the money, perhaps at the end of his life he was paying for his freedom, just as when a young man he chose the provinces rather than the city.

This humble condition which Lotto deliberately assumed, as well as his religious tendencies and singular vision, explain the extraordinary results he achieved as a precursor of pictorial movements. Perhaps too much has been said about this: when reading his critics one finds names like Goya, Delacroix, Manet, Degas, constantly invoked. Undoubtedly Lotto's art is rich with anticipation, though it can also unexpectedly, here and there, revert to the archaic, as for instance in the *Madonna Nursing the Christ Child* (plate 104), which some critics claim was copied from an original by Lazzaro Bastiani. Thus Lotto has been called both a precursor and a late-comer, a Late Gothic and a pre-Baroque. Such a range of definitions is acceptable as homage to his individuality and creative power, but Berenson is right in saying that in Lotto what is old and what is new coexist peacefully, in separate layers and with no contradiction.

The discouragement that dampens the entire "Book of Accounts" (the extraordinary activities recorded in it are puzzling), may possibly justify some claims that at first seem baseless. As he grew older and more depressed, Lorenzo Lotto seems to have become more and more hesitant; his nature was sensitive, somewhat passive and easily available to every appeal and suggestion—so that he was constantly exposed to the danger of eclecticism. This makes him a disconcerting and elusive, if compelling, figure. At times one cannot help wishing again that the "Book of Accounts" had never come to light, for it would then be less difficult to analyze his works. As it is, the document is so biographically rich that it becomes a screen between us and Lotto's art. The querulous man overshadows the artist.

But the old painter could still, at times, regain his powers and produce something as fine as *The Presentation in the Temple* at Loreto (plate 206). It is reasonable to assume that this was his last work and since he did not finish it, its interest is redoubled. His means are now all directed to essential truths, at a time when the tired artist left more to be done by Camillo Bagazzotti and Durante da Caldarola whose work is evident in *The Baptism of Christ* (see comment on plate 201). Painted with the colors of autumn leaves, the figures are grouped around a table (the legs terminating curiously in a design of human feet) against a background of unadorned alcoves, still reminiscent of Bramantino after fifty long years. The influence of those Roman days had never disappeared, for one can list at length Bramante-like qualities in Lotto's architectural elements: among them the Bergamo *Intarsias*, the predella of *The St Lucy Altarpiece* (plates 156 and 159), *Christ Leaving the Hall of Judgment* (plate 216)—authoritatively attributed to Lotto by Longhi.

"So that I should wander no more in my old age I have decided to appease my life in this Holy Place." The artist wrote this in September 1554, when he became an oblate member of the Santa Casa at Loreto, a place he had first come across sixty years before and had never stopped revisiting. Loreto was his country of adoption. He had been living there, now, for two years; he had taken all his goods and paintings with him. He was tired, but went on working. New apprentices were always arriving at his workshop to be met by an old artist who was as mean and neurotic as ever—as indeed is proved by the continual changing of assistants. But as he reluctantly paid out a few *scudi* to Durante da Caldarola, he planned new works of considerable importance, such as *The De Amicis Altarpiece* for Jesi, now unfortunately lost.

He meticulously recorded his expenses, but the last entry

is charitable and moving: he sent four gold *scudi* to the servant-girl who had looked after him during his illness at Venice ten years before, in the home of his friend, Bartolomeo Carpan, a jeweler.

While persisting in his miserly habits, Lotto was gradually detaching himself from the world and everything he had so passionately loved for seventy-six years. His contempt for the world had become final (he had even lost his voice). We may perhaps imagine him reading from Marcus Aurelius: "Soon thou shalt be ashes and bones, and only a name, and perhaps not even a name. A name is but noise, but a vain resonance."

Lotto must have agreed with the Emperor. Twenty-five years earlier Treviso had acclaimed the artist as *pictor celeberrimus* and now, at sixty-five, he was forced to leave that same city because "art could not provide me with enough to pay for my keep." He died in the anonymous peace of a Marches cloister, forgotten by all: the man who had given as no other had, a voice and an image to the contrite, apprehensive, and tormented feeling of that age of opulence and cruelty.

BIOGRAPHICAL NOTES

1480 (about). Lorenzo Lotto is born, probably in Venice, the son of Tommaso, a merchant. The date is inferred from his last will and testament of 1546 in which the artist states that he is "aged approximately sixty-six years." His place of birth has been much discussed; some have suggested that he came from Bergamo or Treviso, but he has been repeatedly described as Venetian and there is no valid reason for doubting this.

1503–06. He lives and works at Treviso.

1503, AUGUST 23. He is asked to evaluate an altarpiece.

1503, SEPTEMBER 6. He appears as a witness in a trial.

1505, APRIL 7. In a document drawn up in his home, he is called "a most outstanding artist" ("*in domo habitationis mo. Laurentii Loti de Venetiis pictoris celeberrimi*").

1506, OCTOBER 18. About to leave Treviso, he promises to pay Agostino Bono sixteen gold ducats for his own expenses and those of his apprentice, Domenico. In the meanwhile he pawns his personal clothing to Agostino.

1506, JUNE 20. Contract with the Prior of San Domenico at Recanati for a *Last Supper*. This work was either lost or never executed.

1507, NOVEMBER 10. The parish priest of Santa Cristina al Tivarone asks Bartolomeo da Bologna, woodcarver, to carve a frame for Lotto's altarpiece.

1508, AUGUST 13. Acting on behalf of Lotto, a notary makes out a warrant against the parish priest of Santa Cristina for a cartload of wine to be seized and held "*pro resto vigore mercedis.*"

1509. Lotto is in Rome, decorating the Vatican's "upper rooms, next to the upper library," that is to say, the *Stanze*. Two receipts of March 9 and September 18 have been found, in which the artist declares that he is from Treviso ("*Magister Laurentius Lottus de Trivisio confessus recepisse. . . .*") Nothing remains or is known of his work in Rome, or of how long he stayed there.

1512. Lotto signs the Jesi *Deposition* and continues working in the Marches.

1513, MAY 13. He receives a commission from Alessandro Martinengo for an altarpiece destined for the Dominican Church of Santo Stefano at Bergamo. He remains in Bergamo with practically no interruptions until 1526 (though in 1525 he is known to have gone to the Spiaggia delle Case Bruciate at Venice). In the same period he must also have gone to the Marches and perhaps to Rome.

29

1526, JANUARY 26. Lotto is in Venice, living in the Monastery of San Giovanni e Paolo.

1526, AUGUST and SEPTEMBER. The archives of the Church of Santa Maria Maggiore show that Lotto is back in Bergamo. The three first payments for the drawings of the Church's *Intarsias* were made at Bergamo (1523, 1524, 1525); the rest (1527, January, August, September, and June 1530) were made at Venice.

1531, SEPTEMBER. Titian, Bonifacio and Lotto are appointed trustees of a fund left by Vincenzo Catena to provide dowries for the daughters of impoverished artists.

1530–42. Lotto lives chiefly in Venice, but he journeys to the Marches, to Treviso (August 29, 1532), to Jesi—where he executes frescoes, now lost, in the Palazzo Pubblico (1535)—to Ancona where, on November 11, 1538, he starts his "Book of Accounts" which is kept up to date until 1556. On July 3, 1540, he is living in the home of his nephew, Mario d'Armano, at Venice.

1542, MARCH 28. Lotto finishes the *St Antoninus Altarpiece* for the Dominican Friars of San Giovanni e Paolo. In his will he leaves the Convent an agreed sum of thirty-five ducats on condition that the friars provide him, on his death, with a free burial and that he be interred wearing a monk's habit. "The remainder, amounting to thirty-five ducats, shall have to meet, at my death, all the expenses of my body's burial, clad in religious garments, and placed to rest in one of their tombs." This clause is repeated in Lotto's last will and testament of 1546.

1542, OCTOBER 18. The artist leaves Venice and goes to live at Treviso in the home of Ioan del Saon, ". . . wanting to get away from home because of the many disturbances and going to Treviso to have a quieter life."

1544, OCTOBER. He is asked to evaluate an altarpiece by Francesco Beccaruzzi for the Church of Santa Maria di Valdobbiadene.

1544, NOVEMBER. He is assisted in the execution of a painting by Girolamo da Santacroce.

1545, DECEMBER 12. Lotto leaves Treviso for a number of reasons, but mainly because "art could not provide me with enough to pay for my keep," and returns to Venice where he sets up house in the Rialto, near "San Mathia."

1546, MARCH 25. He draws up a new will at Venice, in which he appoints as executors "my fathers and brothers in Christ, the Governors of the Hospital of San Zuane Polo [San Giovanni e Paolo]." He leaves tools, money and personal effects to two young artists "who are to take as their wives two girls of a quiet nature, healthy in body and mind." He apologizes for not mentioning in the will "any relatives or people of my own blood, because they are few and well provided for." He bequeathes the sum of ten ducats to "Donna Lucia Cadorina, a washerwoman at San Moyse in Corte de Cha Barozi, or to her son, Ioan Maria, who is now about ten years old: this is because she has been faithful to me in the Charity of Christ."

1546, autumn. Lotto is ill in the home of his friend, the jeweler Bartolomeo Carpan who, with the women of his household "cared for me very well for about a month and a half."

1547, NOVEMBER. He stays in Carampane until the following summer.

1548, JUNE 16. He goes to live in one of the houses belonging to the Contarini family in the area of "San Zuan degolao."

1549, MAY 15. Lotto leaves Venice for good, entrusting some cameos and paintings to Sansovino "on account and in order to raise money from them."

1549, JULY 1. He goes to Ancona to paint an altarpiece for San Francesco delle Scale. At first he lives in the Church, then rents a house from Hieronimo Scalamonti "behind San Pietro," and orders several repairs and alterations.

1550, AUGUST. On the occasion of the Holy Year, Lotto organizes a lottery of thirty of his paintings, but succeeds in selling only seven. Instead of the 400 *scudi* he had hoped to raise, he obtains 39 *scudi* and 29 *bolognini*.

1552, AUGUST 30. He goes to the Santa Casa at Loreto and is received by the Governor. "I have been given a room, and a place in which to work, and there will be food for me and my assistant. I shall be allowed to accept work

from others for my own profit and also to do some work for the good of my conscience."

1554, SEPTEMBER 8. Lotto becomes an oblate in the Santa Casa: "So that I should wander no more in my old age I have decided to appease my life in this Holy Place. I have become an oblate for the rest of my life and given myself with all my goods to this Home which will provide me always with all I need of food and clothing."

1556, SEPTEMBER 1. He sends four gold *scudi* to the jeweler, Bartolomeo Carpan, at Venice, having "promised that sum to Carpan's housekeeper in the event of her marriage."

1556, autumn? Lorenzo Lotto dies at Loreto. If his death occurred later, it still must have been some time before the following date which is self-explanatory.

1557, JULY 1. A receipt discovered by Gianuizzi, mentions a small sum of money paid to the Santa Casa "for the mattress that used to belong to Lorenzo Lotto which had to be sold to the French."

From the many detailed items of information contained in the "Book of Accounts" we list below those relating to the remarkable succession of apprentices who passed through Lotto's workshop during the last nomadic years of the artist's life.

1542. At Venice and later, in 1549, on "Bernardin, my assistant" of whom nothing else is known.

1547, JANUARY 29. He engages in Venice "Piero de Cenetia, the son of Dona Orsola." The next year, on September 26 "I peacefully rid myself of him, as we could not stand each other."

1548, SEPTEMBER 27. He engages "Isepo, a painter from Poltrenga de Bergamo," who stays with him until August 20, 1550. "I pay him no salary; only his expenses and what he needs to be decently attired."

1549, APRIL 1. He employs "Paolo of Brescia, the son of Zan Francesco Rosino, a doctor of medicine in Brescia." Paolo stays with Lotto until February 18, 1550, and the artist pays for a friar "to instruct him in things spiritual and in the sacraments of the Church."

1550, AUGUST 25. In Ancona he engages "Ioan Mateo, a painter from Pesaro."

1550, SEPTEMBER 9. He engages "Marcho of Fiume, formerly known as Zorzi Catalenich, whom I believe to be about fourteen years old." He dismisses him on December 27 "because his nature cannot be tamed."

1550, DECEMBER. He engages "Hercule (Ramazzani) de la Rocha Contrada" and succeeds in keeping him until November 1552, when having "lost patience with that young man's disproportionate nature, I removed him from my sight." On that occasion he stated to the Governor at Loreto that "I want to instruct apprentices no longer, for they are ungrateful. The moment they have learned something they leave me."

1553, AUGUST 10. Lotto tries again with "Simon, the son of Master Ioan Andrea, a painter from Caldarola." The results were meager. The boy "stayed only eight days."

1553, AUGUST. A new attempt, with Paolo da San Genesio. "He stayed about twenty days and was paid two *scudi*. He stole approximately three *scudi*."

1553, SEPTEMBER 23. Lotto employs "Paolo, the son of Master Andrea, a mason from Lombard." He dismissed him in December for his "haughty nature and bad manners."

1554, JANUARY 26. His last attempt: "Bastiano, a painter and the son of Master Baptista de San Jenese, also a painter, offered his services; . . . on January 29 he left and took with him my pouch of money, shirts, new boots, handkerchiefs, my belt, a fine black hat and books for a total value of about six *scudi*."

This concludes the turnover of Lotto's apprentices. At this point the old artist, who now probably only painted a little, decided to work alone. Occasionally, however, he found a few assistants.

1550, APRIL 12. Durante, an artist from Caldarola, who had previously helped Lotto with the Mogliano *Madonna in Glory*, came to assist the artist at Ancona, and was paid on May 13, 1551. On July 11 of the same year, Durante went again to stay with Lotto, but left him on August 10 to "go and see his mother who was ill." Lotto paid him "two gold *scudi*, one of which was partly worn, and the other rusty." Durante "promised to come back in good time, but did not return." We are not surprised.

1553. During this year, Antonuzzo of Jesi helped Lotto with *The De Amicis Altarpiece* (see "Lost Works") from July 2 until December 9. When the work was finished, however, he asked for leave to go home, for his wife wanted a child.

1554, NOVEMBER 29. Camillo Bagazzotti of Camerino, Lotto's last assistant, is paid a salary. In 1555, as shown in the accounts of the Santa Casa at Loreto, Bagazzotti is paid twenty-four *scudi* for having assisted Lotto (according to Gianuizzi).

LOTTO'S PAINTINGS

Color Plate I

MADONNA AND CHILD WITH SAINTS. Detail of plate 1a.

Plate 1a

MADONNA AND CHILD WITH SAINTS. *Panel,* 55×87.* *Naples, Pinacoteca Nazionale.* Signed and dated (on the reverse side) 1503. The Saints represented are Peter Martyr and the Infant John the Baptist. Biscaro suggests that this work was executed at Treviso for Bishop Bernardo de'Rossi (plate 3)—originally depicted in place of the Infant St John—as an act of thanksgiving for escape, in September 1503, from a plot to assassinate him. The substitution, previously spotted by Crowe and Cavalcaselle, is fairly obvious; a cross once held by the effaced suppliant is still visible. The scheme is in Giovanni Bellini's tradition, with its focal center shifted to the right. A series of X-rays carried out in 1953 at Venice has revealed nothing but blots under St John, proving that the original figure must have been erased.

Plate 1b

SACRA CONVERSAZIONE. *Panel,* 85×100. *Edinburgh, National Gallery of Scotland, on loan from the Earl of Ellesmere Collection.* Signed, and executed about 1505. Coletti has published a replica of this work at Dresden.

Plate 2

PORTRAIT OF A YOUTH. *Panel,* 29×23. *Florence, Uffizi.* Executed about 1505, as suggested by Boschetto because of the painting's Northern peculiarities reminiscent of Dürer and de'Barbari. Coletti, on the other hand, thinks it was painted at the end of the Bergamo period, but this seems unlikely. Several *pentimenti* suggest that this work was painted over an earlier picture. (This opinion was stated orally by the well-known Italian expert, M. Pellicioli, restorer of Da Vinci's *Last Supper* at Milan.)

Plate 3

PORTRAIT OF BISHOP BERNARDO DE'ROSSI. *Panel,* 34.5×42. *Naples, Pinacoteca Nazionale.* Executed in 1505. Variously ascribed to Holbein, G. Bellini and J. de'Barbari, but attributed to Lotto as early as 1680 in an inventory at Parma. The attribution was later published by Biscaro. The portrait shows strict adherence to Antonello da Messina's style, and is one of the masterpieces of Lotto's Treviso period. However, the beautiful green curtain rippling with pleats, and the thin strip of sky are new elements, suggesting Northern influences.

Plate 4

ALLEGORICAL SCENE. *Panel,* 56×43. *Washington, D.C., National Gallery of Art (S. H. Kress Collection).* Executed in 1505. After undergoing

* All dimensions are given in centimeters.

many misfortunes (for a time it was even thought lost), this panel was recently given by the S. H. Kress Foundation to the National Gallery of Art in Washington, D.C. It served as the cover of Bishop de' Rossi's portrait (plate 3) and is inscribed on the back: BERNARDUS RUBEUS / BERCETI COMES PONTIF TARVIS. / AETAT. ANN. XXX VI MENSE X.D.V. / LAURENTIUS LOTTUS P. / CAL. IUL. MDV. The landscape, which includes a shipwreck, stresses the contrast between serenity and storm. It may be considered a forerunner of the altarpiece for the Church of the Carmini (plate 133), painted twenty-five years later.

Plate 5

A MAIDEN'S DREAM. *Panel, 45 × 33. Washington, D.C., National Gallery of Art.* Discovered at the end of the nineteenth century by Lord Conway at Milan; Kress Gift No. 268 to the National Gallery in Washington. In 1905, Berenson suggested the landscape was German or Lombard rather than Venetian, and that the whole was one of Lotto's less mature works. With good reason, Coletti—who changed the title of the work from *Danaë* into its present one, since the Cupid is showering petals, not gold, on the reclining maiden—dates it about 1505, bringing it close in time to the *Allegorical Scene* (plate 4) and the Louvre's *St Jerome in the Wilderness* (plate 10).

Plate 6

BUST OF A WOMAN. *Panel, 36 × 28. Dijon, Museum.* Executed about 1505–06. Attributed to Lotto by Frizzoni; previously catalogued as by Dürer or Holbein. The painting is remarkable for its subtle modulation of coloring.

Plate 7

THE ASSUMPTION OF THE VIRGIN. *Panel, 175 × 162. Asolo, Parish Church.* Signed and dated: LAURENT. LOTUS / IUNIOR M.D.VI. The word *junior* is inexplicable unless, as Crowe and Cavalcaselle, and Berenson, one reads it as *junii*. The Virgin's archaic and austere appearance contrasts with the fervid expression of the two Saints (Anthony Abbot and Louis of Toulouse). The beautiful landscape, on the other hand, recalls those of Northern prints. Longhi finds that these contrasts evoke "a new world"; he also attributes to Lotto the *Dead Christ* at the top of the altarpiece and landscape of the predella (plate 214), but the former is too low in quality, and the predella, though its conception and light effects are good, is larger in treatment than the three figures. Longhi's theory, based on the assumption that the top and predella were painted a considerable time before the main panel, is therefore hard to accept. Coletti, who rejects it, conjectures that before leaving the Marches, Lotto asked the framemaker to finish the work "providing him, perhaps, with a rough sketch or two." Coletti concedes "some grace and refinement" in the quail, seen with a lobster and a butterfly in the foreground of the landscape. The perspective and design of the landscape however, remind C. Sterling of Lotto's wood *Intarsias* (reported in conversation). Other critics including Fiocco, have mentioned the possible authorship of Lazzaro Bastiani. (See also plate 8.)

Plate 8

THE ASSUMPTION OF THE VIRGIN. Detail of landscape, with scroll bearing the signature and date.

Plate 9a

THE MARRIAGE OF ST CATHE-
RINE. *Panel, 70 × 90. Munich, Alte
Pinakothek.* Signed, and painted
about 1506. One of the most perfect
works of Lotto's Treviso period.
Against the green curtain the figures
of the Virgin, St Catherine, and the
Child form a pyramidal composition,
the symmetry of which is violently
broken diagonally by St Joseph, and
by the landscape at left, typified by
that very same atmosphere of
impending panic that we find in the
Louvre's *St Jerome in the Wilderness*
(plate 10). A version of the pyramidal
group only is in the Boston Museum
of Fine Arts. A drawing for the
Virgin's head—published by L.
Grassi in *Paragone*, 1954—is in
Rome's Gabinetto Nazionale delle
Stampe. (See also plate 9b.)

Plate 9b

THE MARRIAGE OF ST CATHE-
RINE. Detail: heads of St Catherine
and the Child.

Plate 10

ST JEROME IN THE WILDERNESS.
Panel, 48 × 40. Paris, Louvre. Signed
and dated 1506. Formerly part of
Cardinal Fesch's Collection; in the
Louvre since 1857. The signature
was considered to be false by Crowe
and Cavalcaselle, but genuine by
Morelli. The date used to be read as
1500 but J. Wilde correctly read
(*Burlington Magazine*, 1950) the last
numeral as a six. This has revolu-
tionized early Lotto chronology and
invalidated several theories,
because Giorgione's *Gipsy and Soldier*,
for instance, had undoubtedly been
painted by that date. Berenson finds
Jerome's robes reminiscent of Bellini; Coletti traces the romantic
feeling for nature expressed in the
painting to Altdorfer and the Danube
School. But the chromatic and
luminous depth of the landscape is
typically the work of Lotto. The
same may be said of the crystal-clear
rocks, veined with dry branches and
twigs, and of the Saint beating his
breast, "meditating and taking a sun
cure" (Coletti).

Plate 11

ST JEROME IN THE WILDERNESS.
*Panel, 80.5 × 61. Rome, Castel Sant'
Angelo.* Signed. Painted some time
after the Louvre's *St Jerome*, but
much more generic than the previous
work (plate 10) which has greater
lyrical impetus. This panel comes
from the Menotti Bequest. Its merits
are to be found in the landscape,
broadly conceived and executed in
minute detail.

Plates 12a and b

THE DEAD SAVIOR, *lunette. Panel,
90 × 162.* THE SANTA CRISTINA
ALTARPIECE. *Panel, 177 × 162.
Altarpiece in the Parish Church of Santa
Cristina al Tivarone (Treviso).* Signed.
The work was finished in 1507 and
the last payment was recorded as
made in 1508. It could not have been
executed before Giovanni Bellini's
altarpiece at San Zaccaria in Venice,
since its arrangement resembles
Bellini's, as Berenson and Pignatti
have noted. Pallucchini sees a
"polemical opposition between this
altarpiece and Giorgione's *Castelfranco Madonna.*" Lotto's archaism is
enlivened here by his extraordinary
personal treatment, as in St Cristina's
anxious, pathetic expression (she is
depicted with SS Peter, Liberale and
Jerome), and in the sad, spiritual
Pietà in the lunette with its grieving
Angels.

Plate 13

THE SANTA CRISTINA ALTAR-
PIECE. Detail: the Madonna and
Child.

Plate 14

THE SANTA CRISTINA ALTAR-
PIECE. Detail: St Cristina.

Plate 15

THE SANTA CRISTINA ALTAR-
PIECE. Detail: St Jerome.

Plate 16

BUST OF A YOUTH AGAINST A
WHITE CURTAIN. *Panel, 42.3 ×
35.8. Vienna, Kunsthistorisches Museum.*
About 1506–08. Formerly attributed
to Jacopo de'Barbari and re-
established as a work by Lotto by
Biscaro. The wart on the youth's
forehead like the one on Bishop de'
Rossi's cheek is a statement of Lotto's
realistic portraiture.

Color Plate II

PORTRAIT OF MESSER MARSILIO
AND HIS BRIDE. Detail of plate 69.

Plate 17

MADONNA AND CHILD WITH
SAINTS. *Panel, 53 × 67. Rome,
Borghese Gallery.* Signed and dated
1508. On the right and left of the
Virgin are St Onophrius and a

Bishop Saint. In Berenson's opinion,
the work was executed at Recanati,
and although at first he rejected the
obvious parallel between the hermit
St Onophrius and one of the Elders
in Dürer's panel *Christ Among the
Elders*, he recently admitted that the
figure suggests Dürer. Using vivid
colors against a black background,
Lotto breaks up the apparent symmetry of the composition by pushing
the hermit back into mid-distance
and creating a general air of excite-
ment by means of swift, nervous
lines. The Bishop is offering the
Child his wounded heart. The heart
reappears in the panel depicting *St
Catherine of Siena* in *The Recanati
Polyptych* (plate 24), also completed
in 1508.

Plate 18

BUST OF A DOMINICAN MONK.
*Panel, 32.5 × 25. Upton House,
Banbury, Oxfordshire.* About 1508.
Formerly in the Auspitz Collection
at Vienna and now in the Bearstead
Donation to the National Trust,
Upton House, Banbury. One of the
most subtle portraits painted in this
period. The colors are exquisite:
pink face, ivory-white cowl, and the
usual green curtain. Berenson (1955)
believes this monk to have been the
model for the young Saint in the
Asolo *Assumption of the Virgin* (plate
7).

THE RECANATI POLYPTYCH

(Plates 19–25)]
The polyptych is divided into six
compartments. Of the predella,
described by Vasari as "decorated
with small figures and an object of
rare beauty," only one part is
believed extant and is in Vienna (see

plate 25). Lotto received the commission in 1506 from the friars of
San Domenico at Recanati. The
work is signed and dated 1508. On
June 17, 1506, the Dominicans asked
the *Comune* for a contribution "*pro
chona magni pretii*" that Lotto had

undertaken to paint from drawings he had submitted and which was to be "much better even than the works of his youth or, rather, of his adolescence." Frizzoni, commenting upon this important document published by Gianuizzi, surmises that Lotto had shown the friars some of his early works. Coletti rejects this assumption and suggests that the artist had previously worked in the Marches. This would strengthen the theory that Melozzo da Forlì had played a part in his education.

The polyptych was taken apart in the nineteenth century and re-assembled in 1914 within a fake Renaissance frame, and can be seen today in the art gallery at Recanati. The work is a crowning conclusion of Lotto's first cycle of experiments "stimulated by his argument with Giorgione's tones," in the words of Pallucchini. This scholar also points out the subtle, complex rhythmic qualities within the archaic scheme of the composition. Note also the

remarkably coherent action of light and shadow in the three chief sections.

Plate 19

MADONNA ENTHRONED WITH SAINTS. *Panel, 227 × 108.* Central panel. The Virgin, enthroned between SS Urban and Gregory, hands a robe to an Angel who presents it to St Dominic. The tiaras of the two Popes, practically touching the paneled arch, are the starting-points of two diagonals, the key lines of the composition. One of them is picked up, slightly off-center, by the two small surprised Angels with viol and rebec, moving away from the kneeling St Dominic. But animating the whole scene is the light, dancing here and there, but coherently directed. (See also plate 20.)

Plate 20

MADONNA ENTHRONED WITH SAINTS. Detail: the musical Angels.

Plate 21

PIETÀ. *Panel, 80 × 108.* Top panel. Here Lotto achieves sublime intensity in the cramped and broken lines around the great nude torso, in the Angel's sad profile as he looks at the Virgin (her sleeves curiously rich and pleated) who holds the Savior's lifeless hand. From the dark background, the aged Nicodemus gazes at the scene much as he might in a panel by Dürer; at right, Mary Magdalen peers out from her midnight-blue cloak. The colors are varied, from the Angel's yellow and purple to the pink, purple, and blue of the Virgin.

Plate 22

SS THOMAS AQUINAS AND FLAVIAN. *Panel, 155 × 67.* Lower left wing of the polyptych. The beautiful black-and-white display of the

Dominican woolen habit of St Thomas, painted with an assured sense of plasticity, reveals how strong Antonello da Messina's influence was on Lotto.

Plate 23

SS PETER MARTYR AND VITUS. *Panel, 155 × 67.* Lower right wing of the polyptych. Note the contrast between the curls, ribbons, and shoulder-knots of the obese St Vitus, protector of Recanati, and the black-and-white austerity of his Dominican companion.

Plate 24a

SS CATHERINE OF ALEXANDRIA AND VINCENT FERRER. *Panel, 67 × 67.* The two couples of Saints —at half-length—are seen in the upper wings, outside the polyptych's architectural frame. On the left are SS Catherine of Alexandria and Vincent Ferrer. The former is a human type which appears frequently in this painting: a circular, flattened face with a suspicion of goitre. The Angel in the top panel's *Pietà* has the same face (plate 21).

Plate 24b

SS CATHERINE OF SIENA AND SIGISMUND. *Panel, 67 × 67.* As in the other panels a Dominican Saint in black-and-white is opposed to a Saint painted in bright colors. Here, the aristocratic St Sigismund, painted in brown and gold, with his beautiful, languorous hand offers a striking contrast to the fat Saint from Siena, depicted clasping her heart.

Plate 25

A DOMINICAN SAINT PREACHING. *Panel, 24 × 61. Vienna, Kunsthistorisches Museum (Benda Bequest).* This work seems to fit Vasari's description of one of the three predella panels: "St Dominic preaching, with some of the most graceful small figures in the world." Though undoubtedly beautiful, the panel is, however, more mature, and does not coincide with the rest of the polyptych. Venturi rightly notes that here, as in the later *St Lucy Altarpiece* at Jesi, "Lorenzo Lotto appears as the only perpetuator in sixteenth-century Venice of Vittor Carpaccio, whose technique he carries to its limit, until it reaches the threshold of modern Impressionism." Berenson (1955) also attributed to Lotto two *Sketches of Monks Preaching* in the Museo Civico at Bassano, one of which is closer to the Vienna panel; the subject of the other is the *Confirmation of the Dominican Order*, perhaps destined for the same predella.

Plate 26a

HOLY FAMILY WITH ST GABRIEL. *Canvas, 73 × 63. Princeton University Museum, New Jersey.* Signed and dated 1512. Formerly in the Tadini Oratory at Romano Lombardo (Bergamo). Coletti infers, therefore, that Lotto had contacts with that region of Italy as early as 1512. Pignatti suggests that this date is based on the Venetian Calendar and should in fact be read as 1513. The work recalls Mantegna and Correggio.

Plate 26b

SACRA CONVERSAZIONE. *Panel, 40 × 29. Formerly at Krakow, in Count Sigismund Puslowski's Collection.* Signed and datable about 1508. Berenson points out elements and figures recalling *The Recanati Polyptych.*

Plate 27a

ST VINCENT FERRER IN GLORY. *Detached fresco, 265 × 166. Recanati, Church of San Domenico.* Executed about 1512–13. Mentioned by Vasari. Like the *putti* in *The Deposition* (plate 28), the Cherubs are Raphaelesque. The colors of this fresco are magnificent: a transparent breath of pink hovers above a stern blend of ocher and gray.

Plate 27b

ST JAMES THE PILGRIM. *Panel, 20 × 15. Recanati, Church of Santa Maria sopra Mercanti.* About 1512–13. This work is warm with delightful browns and reds.

Plate 28

THE DEPOSITION. *Panel, 298 × 198. Jesi, Pinacoteca.* Signed and dated 1512. After his fruitless—as far as we know—visit to Rome, Lotto returned to the Marches where he shows the first signs of his artistic contacts with Rome, particularly with Raphael, who is far too present in this cumbersome composition. Lotto here reaches a crisis in his development.

Confronted with such disorderly excesses, Venturi wrote: "We have the impression that when Lorenzo Lotto's personality came into direct contact with Raphael's art, it ran into difficulty." However, the spatial clarity of the landscape partly redeems the inane and overdone expression of the figures. The work is interesting as an example of a momentary cultural impasse for Lotto; he was usually immune to such dangers. Berenson (1955) records a studio version of the Jesi *Deposition*, partly by the artist's own hand, in the Biandra Collection at Milan. This canvas (149 × 117) was later published by Zampetti in *Arte Veneta*, 1956, p. 183.

Plate 29

THE TRANSFIGURATION. *Arched panel, 300 × 203. Recanati, Pinacoteca.*

Signed LAURENTIUS . . . and datable about 1513. Formerly in the Church of Santa Maria at Castelnuovo, where it was seen by Vasari who described it together with the predella in three parts: one, since lost, portrayed *Christ Praying in the Garden*; the other two are reproduced in the following plates. A wayward breeze seems to agitate the mannered composition, described by Berenson as "characteristic of Lotto's less careful work." The figures, their names inscribed beneath each of them, roll about in large masses.

Plate 30

CHRIST LEADING THE APOSTLES TO MOUNT TABOR. *Panel, 27 × 58. Leningrad, Hermitage.* This and the following panel are from *The Transfiguration* predella (plate 29). Established as Lotto's work by Frizzoni in 1916.

Plate 31

THE ASSUMPTION OF THE VIRGIN. *Panel, 27 × 58. Milan, Brera Gallery.* About 1513. One of the three panels from *The Transfiguration* at Recanati (plate 29). Formerly in the Mattei Collection at Rome, the work then passed from the Oggioni Collection to the Brera (1855). Previously attributed to Raphael and re-established as a Lotto by Frizzoni (1916). Observe the Apostle on the right, about to place his glasses on his nose.

Plate 32a

ST JEROME IN THE WILDERNESS. *Panel, 55 × 43. Sibiu (Rumania), (formerly Hermannstadt), Bruckenthal Gallery.* Signed and executed about 1515. This work is an example of Lotto's Expressionism. The Saint is stretched diagonally across the rough landscape. How remote from the contemplative Jerome of 1506 (plate 10).

Plate 32b

ST JEROME PENITENT. *Canvas, 41 × 33. Allentown, Pennsylvania, Museum of Art (S. H. Kress Collection).* Signed and dated 1515. Lotto returns again to a beloved theme but, were it not for his signature, one would hesitate to accept his authorship of this cumbersome figure. Berenson reports another version of this composition in the Sandor Lederer Collection at Budapest.

Color Plate III

THE LEGEND OF ST BARBARA. Detail of folded reproduction.

Plate 33a

DEAD CHRIST SUPPORTED BY TWO ANGELS. *Panel, 15 × 19. London, formerly in the Benson Collection.* About 1515. Venturi compares this tiny panel with *The Santo Stefano Altarpiece* and finds in it "... a surprising beauty of light colors, the pink and mauve of petals, the tender green of leaves." The background is golden.

Plate 33b

PORTRAIT OF A MAN WITH A ROSARY. *Panel, 78.5 × 62. Nivaagaard (Copenhagen), Hage Collection.* Executed about 1515–20. Formerly in Casa Coccapani at Modena, where it was thought to be by Holbein. Claimed as a Lotto by Morelli and dated by Frizzoni about 1512, but opinion is now unanimous in assigning it to the Bergamo period. There is still some doubt about its authorship.

Plate 34a

PORTRAIT OF PIERO SODERINI. *Panel, 54 × 43. Formerly in the Doetsch Collection, London.* About 1512. The attribution is by Berenson and generally accepted; it is based on the theory that Lotto painted this portrait in the Marches before October 1512, when Soderini embarked at Ancona for his exile at Ragusa. Berenson adds that the portrait appears "without a change" in the official life of Soderini published in Padua in 1737, and reports that an original drawing for this head is in the Devonshire Collection at Chatsworth.

Plate 34b

PORTRAIT OF CHRISTOPHER COLUMBUS. *Panel, 91.4 × 81. Formerly part of the J. W. Ellsworth Collection, Chicago.* Signed and dated 1512. The attribution is by Berenson (1955), who notes also that the portrait was bought in Venice for the Chicago Fair in 1891.

Plate 35a

PORTRAIT OF A JEWELER. *Canvas, 77 × 64. Santa Monica, California, Paul J. Getty Collection.* About 1512–13. Time and restorations have hardened and impoverished this work; the landscape on the left has entirely disappeared. The canvas was formerly in the Kaufmann Collection at Berlin, the Goudstikker Collection at Amsterdam, the Koch Collection at Frankfurt-am-Main and went finally to California from Basel (Switzerland).

Plate 35b

PORTRAIT OF AGOSTINO AND NICCOLÒ DELLA TORRE. *Canvas, 85 × 68. London, National Gallery.* Signed and dated 1515. From the Della Torre family of Bergamo, this work passed in 1812 to Count Teodoro Lechi of Brescia and in 1847 to Count Jestetich of Vienna who sold it in 1859, for 124 gold napoleons (about $478.00), to Giovanni Morelli. Four years later it was acquired for the National Gallery who paid Morelli 400 napoleons (about $1,544). Since Agostino Della Torre was a Professor of Medicine at Padua in 1515, Morelli submitted the theory, accepted by Berenson but now rejected by most critics, that the figure of Niccolò was added later in Bergamo. Boschetto points out the uniformity of this beautiful canvas, which has some Raphaelesque echoes and in which Venturi, commenting upon its still life, finds "a Flemish quality, indicating Lotto's return to his Northern masters."

THE SANTO STEFANO ALTARPIECE

(Plates 36–43)

On May 15, 1513, Lotto signed a contract with Alessandro Martinengo (published by Tassi in 1793) in which the donor, wishing to "leave behind him some tangible evidence of his life," entrusts with this work "*Magister Laurentius fil. Thomaxii de Lotis*" to whom he promises 500 gold ducats. The great altarpiece, destined for the Church of Santo Stefano al Fortino (where Michiel saw it) was finished in 1516 and this date can be read next to Lotto's name. The Church having been demolished in 1561, the altarpiece was moved twice and eventually transferred, in 1600, to the Church of San Bartolomeo at Bergamo. In 1749, when the Church was redecorated, the magnificent frame, described as "*coelesti potius quam terestri manu depictam*," and the pediment were "given to a carpenter for the trouble of destroying them and the central panel was given a Louis Quinze frame" (B. Berenson). The three predella panels (plates 38–40) were relegated to the Sacristy in spite of public protest, and only in 1893 did they find a resting-place in the Accademia Carrara at Bergamo. Recently Boschetto published two small figures of Saints (plates 43b and c) and two *tondi* (plates 43d and e) which were probably part of the altarpiece. Our comprehension of this work today must therefore be limited. Morelli saw a model for it in Bergamo—it is now in America—but Frizzoni described the model as a "rough thing" and Longhi states now that it is a copy by G. P. Cavagna.

Plate 36

MADONNA ENTHRONED WITH SAINTS. *Arched panel, 520 × 250. Bergamo, Church of San Bartolomeo.* Central panel of the altarpiece. Signed and dated 1516. After *The Assumption of the Virgin* at Ancona (plate 197) this is considered Lotto's greatest work, although it reflects a

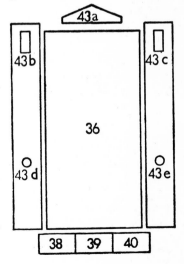

number of influences and is cluttered with subordinate figures (as indeed is the case in Correggio's altarpiece of 1515). The panel sums up Lotto's experiments and Berenson states that its structure is second only to that of Raphael's *School of Athens*. Certainly it does possess a Bramantesque architecture with some elements from Mantegna in the upper part, a fanciful throne in the Ferrara manner and something of Raphael's *Baldacchino Madonna* in the flying Angels. But the distribution and play of the light is exclusively Lotto's and so are the garrulous, nervously lacerated and oblique forms (note the standards above and the golden carpet at the foot of the throne). The tendency is apparent to break the solemn symmetry of the scheme. "Fancy, then, and not geometry" and "a feeling such as the Japanese," as Berenson (1955) so rightly observed, mark the incongruous perspective of the figures in this altarpiece. St Alexander (first on the left) and St Barbara (next to him) are traditionally believed to represent Martinengo and his wife. (See also plate 37.)

Plate 37

MADONNA ENTHRONED WITH SAINTS. Central detail: the Madonna and Child.

Plates 38–40

THE MARTYRDOM OF ST STEPHEN; THE DEPOSITION; MIRACLE OF ST DOMINIC. *Panels, 51 × 97 each. Bergamo, Accademia Carrara.* Predella panels of the altarpiece. It is reasonable to assume that *The Miracle* panel, though certainly conceived by Lotto, was not finished by his own hand, for its quality is greatly inferior to that of the other two scenes which, for their tension of form, chromatic value and daring

feats of light should rank among his masterpieces of the Bergamo period. Venturi sees the influence of Giorgione in *The Martyrdom* and Berenson claims that Lotto would never have painted the "officer in white and purplish colors . . . had he not been acquainted with the works of Giorgione." However, Lotto's language is here, once again, perfectly independent and personal. If we compare this *Deposition* with that of Jesi (plate 28), painted less than four years earlier, we can see how quickly and assuredly the artist had matured since his stay in Rome, once he had come in touch with Northern influences and seen the dramatic value of more violent expression. The casual conversation between two soldiers—one clad in armor, the other half-naked—on the left of *The Martyrdom* (plate 42), the woman in the shadow at the right of *The Deposition*, the backgrounds of classic ruins are all contrasting elements which testify to the dramatic quality of these panels. *The Miracle* especially suggests the same hand that was later to paint the three *Sketches from the Life of Stephen* (plate 215), traditionally assigned to Lotto. (See also plates 41–42.)

Plate 41

THE MARTYRDOM OF ST STEPHEN. Detail: the stoning mob.

Plate 42

THE MARTYRDOM OF ST STEPHEN. Detail: soldiers.

Plate 43a

ANGEL WITH GLOBE AND SCEPTER. *Panel, 46 × 155. Budapest, Museum of Fine Arts.* Formerly in the Piccinelli Collection at Seriate. Originally in the pediment of *The*

Santo Stefano Altarpiece. "This panel, from the Church of San Bartolomeo, was inscribed within an ancient architectural frame, with columns and a triangle at the top, below which a life-size foreshortened Angel leant forward with outstretched arms, holding a crystal globe in one hand. This Angel is truly worthy of this excellent work. In the course of recent alterations, the unintelligent Fathers gave the Angel and the frame to their carpenter. Later it was acquired for eleven lire by one Signor Borsetti who sold it for the sum of two gold coins to Giovanni Ghidini, a priest. On this day, January 2, 1864, I have acquired the said Angel from Signori Pietro and Giuseppe Ghidini, the sons of the late Nicola, whose family were still its rightful owners" (from a marginal note in *Vite dei pittori, scultori e architetti bergamaschi* by F. M. Tassi, made by Antonio Piccinelli di Seriate. The note was published by R. Bassi Rathgeb in *L'Arte*, on June 1, 1959).

Plates 43b and c

ST PETER MARTYR and A DOMINICAN SAINT. *Panels, 54 × 25 each. Florence, R. Longhi Collection.* Boschetto believes them to have been originally inserted between the lower pillars of *The Santo Stefano Altarpiece.*

Plates 43d and e

MARTYRDOM OF ST ALEXANDER and DEAD CHRIST SUPPORTED BY ANGELS. *Wood roundels, diameter 20 each. Raleigh (North Carolina), Museum of Art (S. H. Kress Collection.)* Published by Boschetto and accepted by Berenson. They may have been placed in the original frame of *The Santo Stefano Altarpiece.*

Plate 44

MADONNA AND CHILD WITH FOUR SAINTS. *Panel, 152 × 119. Philadelphia, J. G. Johnson Collection.* About 1517. The archaic setting calls to mind Borgognone (Coletti). This, however, is an isolated work in Lotto's *œuvre.* Berenson, who dates it about 1515, states that the panel has suffered from numerous over-cleanings and restorations.

Plate 45

SUSANNAH AND THE ELDERS. *Canvas, 66 × 50. Florence, Contini-Bonacossi Collection.* Signed and dated 1517. Formerly in the Benson Collection, London. This delightful scene, with a pretty landscape of a Flemish clarity, is bathed in magical light and set on a stage enclosed by a brick wall. Its drama is of the country-comedy type, full of loud talk, wild gestures and scrolls waved about the rather embarrassed actress playing the role of Susannah. An entry in the "Book of Accounts" on January 9, 1548 shows that in his old age the master returned to this theme: "A lifesize Susannah bathing and the two elders portrayed from Nature. . . ." Occasionally small expenses are entered in the book for "asking a woman to undress . . . just to see her. . . ." (See also plate 46.)

Plate 46

SUSANNAH AND THE ELDERS. Detail: landscape at the center.

Plate 47

THE DEPOSITION. *Tempera on canvas, 184 × 184. Bergamo, Church of Sant' Alessandro in Colonna (Sacristy).* About 1517. In very poor condition, but intensely dramatic, the work contains some beautiful details such as the woman in white running with upraised hands towards the dead Savior, and the other one in green kneeling by His feet. An unfortunately small remainder from a masterwork of compelling expressiveness: Berenson, who finds in it anticipations of Jesuit temperament believes it may possibly have been a processional standard.

Plate 48a

VIRGIN NURSING THE CHRIST CHILD. *Panel, 33 × 27. Leningrad, Hermitage.* About 1518–20. A replica, or copy, is in the J. G. Johnson Collection, Philadelphia, published as such by Coletti. Crowe and Cavalcaselle state that the panel, attributed to Cesare da Sesto, has badly deteriorated but does recall Lorenzo Lotto.

Plate 48b

MADONNA AND CHILD WITH THE INFANT ST JOHN. *Panel, 39 × 52. Formerly in the Gemäldegalerie, Dresden.* Signed and dated 1518. Assigned to Lotto by Frizzoni in 1889, before Loeser discovered the signature and date in 1891. With some hints of Raphael in the children, the overall composition is like Leonardo's (Berenson).

Color Plate IV

THE LEGEND OF ST BARBARA. Detail of folded reproduction.

Plate 49a

THE TRINITY. *Canvas, 170 × 115. Bergamo, Church of Sant'Alessandro della Croce (Sacristy).* About 1517. Formerly in the Church of the Trinità, demolished at the end of the eighteenth century. The figure of Christ among the clouds is vaguely pietistic and trite, but the landscape is beautiful.

Plate 49b

CHERUB WITH A SKULL. *Panel, 51 × 52. London, Duke of Northumberland Collection.* About 1520–25, as assumed by Pallucchini who published it as a Lotto in 1951, correcting the attribution to Schedoni, and proclaimed it "an example of Lotto's subtler poetry."

Plate 50

THE SAN BERNARDINO ALTARPIECE. *Canvas, 300 × 275. Bergamo, Church of San Bernardino in Pignolo.* Signed and dated 1521. Lotto, having reached full maturity is here at his most capricious: the unadorned pedestal of the throne is broken by the carpet and by the Angel (a light tobacco-brown) crouching at its foot; two Angels hold up a green curtain behind the red-clad Virgin, and two others spread it into a canopy over her head; reflected light and halfshadows play about the forms, making them unstable and weightless; the two huge Saints on the extreme right and left of the picture, humped and Northern-looking as they are, frame and control the exuberance. At the Ambrosiana in Milan are two preparatory sketches for the figure of Joseph. In pointing out the merits of this splendid work, F. M. Tassi relates that in 1591, when it became known that the monks intended to sell the painting, the local authorities decided to buy it to prevent its being taken away, and for that purpose they appointed two citizens with the task of finding out: "*quomodo sit retinenda in praesenti civitate ad illius decus et ornamentum dicta anchona*" (how the altarpiece might be retained as decoration and ornamentation in the city). (See also plates 51–52.)

Plate 51

THE SAN BERNARDINO ALTAR-
PIECE. Detail: two Angels at right.

Plate 52

THE SAN BERNARDINO ALTAR-
PIECE. Detail: Angel writing at the
foot of the throne.

Plate 53

PORTRAIT OF LUCINA BREM-
BATE. *Panel, 51 × 42. Bergamo,
Accademia Carrara.* About 1520.
Formerly in the Collection of Count
Grumelli at Bergamo. In 1913, Ciro
Caversazzi was able to identify the
sitter from the coat of arms on her
ring and from the conundrum of the
moon in the upper-left corner containing her Christian name (the
letters "CI" in *luna* (moon) forming
the name Lu-Ci-na). There is a
provincial note in the excess of
ornamentation: pearls over her head
and neck; her rings; a jeweled horn
for protection against the evil eye.
Lotto paid excessive attention to
these details. The moonlit landscape
completes a work that is richly
painted.

Plate 54

THE SANTO SPIRITO ALTAR-
PIECE. *Canvas, 287 × 269. Bergamo,
Church of Santo Spirito.* Signed and
dated 1521. "It avoids the mistakes
of the San Bernardino altarpicce
[plate 50], but it has neither its
freshness nor its depth of feeling"
(Berenson). The garland of Angels
flying above the throne evokes again
Correggio whose Cupola at Parma
was finished at least five years after
this canvas. Zampetti writes: "No
artist at that moment of the history of
classic art would have ever thought
of painting his Angels green or
pink, like feathers of various colors

floating around in space. . . ." (See
also plate 55.)

Plate 55

THE SANTO SPIRITO ALTAR-
PIECE. Detail: the Infant St John at
the foot of the throne.

Plate 56

CHRIST TAKING LEAVE OF HIS
MOTHER. *Canvas, 126 × 99. Berlin,
Staatliches Museen.* Signed and dated
1521. From the placid Italian garden,
the broken evening light invades the
magnificent Renaissance hall, painted
"with the subtlety of Vermeer Van
Delft" (Berenson): the atmosphere
heightens the pathos. The scene is a
document of a number of Lotto's
stylistic tendencies: an echo of
Correggio, a foretaste of Counter-
Reformation, a shade of Northern
sentimentality and Expressionism. In
1648, Ridolfi saw this painting in
the house of Domenico Tassi at
Bergamo, and stated that the woman
on the right is Elizabetta Rotta,
Domenico's wife. Tassi himself was
portrayed in a like canvas, depicting
a *Nativity*; a copy is in the Accademia
at Venice (Berenson is not sure if it
might not be the original). A similar
Nativity was seen by Michiel in the
home of Domenico del Cornello at
Bergamo and Vasari reports yet
another in the house of Tomaso da
Empoli at Florence: all these paintings were "nocturnal." Lotto's
feeling for light is rarely so subtly
and thoughtfully expressed. Compare the beautiful clear sky seen
through the arches, with the dimmer
light coming through the round
window above like an enormous
moon suspended in empty space.
The white rabbits with raised ears
in the far ground act as a small
counterpoint to the whole scene.
(See also plates 57–58.)

Plate 57

CHRIST TAKING LEAVE OF HIS MOTHER. Detail: the women supporting the Virgin.

Plate 58

CHRIST TAKING LEAVE OF HIS MOTHER. Detail: the background.

Plate 59

MADONNA AND CHILD WITH SAINTS. *Panel, 82 × 118. Florence, Contini-Bonacossi Collection.* Signed and executed about 1521. The work comes from the Convent of Santa Grata, Bergamo. The colors are intense and the composition strangely disturbing, the perspective especially. Berenson observes that the worshippers, SS Rock and Sebastian, are supposedly placed "at some distance below and looking up at the Madonna whose foreshortening is thus explained." Coletti has observed that here Lotto "anticipates the indifference to perspective peculiar to the Mannerists." "The painting in the possession of the Nuns of Santa Grata was sold by them for a low price to the priest, Giovanni Ghidini, a short time before the extinction of their Order in 1798. On this day, February 2, 1864, I have acquired it from the Ghidini brothers, sons of the late Nicola and of whom the said priest Giovanni was a great-uncle. It is in excellent condition, signed by the artist and one of his finest works . . ." (from a marginal note by A. Piccinelli. See comment on plate 43a).

Plate 60

MADONNA AND CHILD WITH SAINTS. *Panel, 88 × 71. London, National Gallery (Colnaghi Bequest, 1908).* Signed and dated 1521. The Saints are Jerome and Anthony of Padua. The composition is typical of Lotto, and he repeated it the following year in the Costa di Mezzate *Madonna.* (See plate 61.)

Plate 61

MADONNA AND CHILD WITH TWO SAINTS. *Canvas, 74 × 68. Costa di Mezzate (Bergamo), Camozzi Collection.* Signed and dated 1522. Tassi reports having seen it in the Pezzoli house at Bergamo. Notice the squirrel on St Catherine's arm, bright with color, as indeed is the whole painting. In Venturi's opinion, this work approaches the highest Venetian art. The figure on the Virgin's left is St John the Baptist.

Plate 62

ST CATHERINE OF ALEXANDRIA. *Panel, 57 × 50. Washington, D.C., National Gallery of Art (S. H. Kress Collection).* Signed and dated 1522. Formerly at Leningrad (St Petersburg) in the Leuchtenberg Collection. A variant of this panel, in the Poldi-Pezzoli Museum in Milan, is considered by some scholars to be an old copy. There are many others; one, recorded by Tassi in the Pozzi house at Bergamo, passed to Lisbon in 1753.

Plate 63

THE NATIVITY. *Panel, 46 × 36. Washington, D.C., National Gallery of Art (S. H. Kress Collection).* Signed and dated 1523. Formerly in the Morlani Collection at Bergamo.

Plate 64

THE MARRIAGE OF ST CATHERINE. *Canvas, 172 × 134. Bergamo, Accademia Carrara.* Signed and dated 1523. Seen by Michiel in the house of Niccolò Bonghi at Bergamo, we have it on his authority that the male figure behind the chair on the left is Niccolò himself. This is one of Lotto's most eloquent hymns in praise of feminine beauty and elegance. The good taste he reveals in the choice of materials calls to mind Veronese (Crowe and Cavalcaselle). Unfortunately, a beautiful landscape of Mount Sinai, originally painted in the blank space above the parapet, was cut out and carried away by a French soldier in 1527. Berenson feels the composition is also marred by the obtrusive presence of Bonghi, whose portrait, however, is most effective. (See also plates 65–66.)

Plate 65

THE MARRIAGE OF ST CATHERINE. Detail: donor, Niccolò Bonghi.

Plate 66

THE MARRIAGE OF ST CATHERINE. Detail: the Madonna and Child.

Plate 67

THE MARRIAGE OF ST CATHERINE. *Canvas, 98 × 113.5. Rome, Galleria Nazionale.* Signed and dated 1524. Formerly in the Quirinale where it was catalogued as by Correggio. In a bill published by Locatelli (see also comment on plate 69) one reads: "The painting for the room of Messer Ma rilio (the bridegroom of the Madridspicture), and in the center the Madonna, with the Child in her arms...." Then all the other Saints are listed, at so much per figure; in order to achieve a round sum the lion of St Jerome is priced with St Sebastian who is no more than a bust. The total due is fifty-three lire. A dazzling painting, Crowe and Cavalcaselle consider it among Lotto's best works. The right side of the canvas compels particular attention: especially the sensual Catherine and her refined and detailed clothing: for instance, the belt clasped by a medallion showing a Cherub holding a pair of scales (visible also in plate 166), and a precious ornament hanging from it, adorned with a sacred heart. Rays of intense light fall on her fingernails, on the bell and book of St Anthony Abbot and on the haloes, their luminosity no longer uniform. (See also plate 68.)

Plate 68

THE MARRIAGE OF ST CATHERINE. Detail: St Catherine.

Plate 69

PORTRAIT OF MESSER MARSILIO AND HIS BRIDE. *Canvas, 71 × 84. Madrid, Prado.* Signed and dated 1523. Again, from the bill published by Locatelli (see comment on plate 67): "The picture with the portraits of Messer Marsilio and his bride, and a small Cupid, and for painting those clothes in simulated silk, and those necklaces, L.30." Berenson states that the color scheme is "almost a gray monochrome such as we frequently find in Lotto ten or fifteen years later," and observes that this is perhaps the "first positively humorous interpretation of characters and situations in Italian painting." Frizzoni, commenting on the laurel-wreathed yoke with which Cupid performs the marriage, writes: "With this allegory the artist intended to show how his own nature was aloof from the bonds of conjugal life." Perhaps Frizzoni was taking too much for granted.

Plate 70

DOUBLE PORTRAIT. *Canvas, 98 × 118. Formerly in Berlin, R. Lepke Collection.* About 1523–25. Formerly at Gatschina Castle; sold at Lepke's on June 4, 1929, the work has since disappeared. Berenson's information was that the Russians had presumably bought it back. Boschetto believes it to be in fact a Lotto canvas now at Antwerp called: *Cavalier and His Bride with Little Dog* (Ridolfi). A preparatory sketch hangs in the Rijksmuseum at Amsterdam and a replica, possibly by Lotto himself, has been recorded by Berenson at Bergamo.

datable about 1523-25. Boschetto suggests a much later date of execution, such as 1547, and the "Book of Accounts" contains a reference to a family portrait of Messer Zuane (Giovanni) della Volta, with his wife and two children, painted that year. Boschetto's theory, rejected by Coletti, is endorsed by Berenson, who writes, "It is clear from the woman's dress that it could not have been painted earlier than 1540." (See also plate 72.)

Plate 71

FAMILY GROUP. *Canvas, 115 × 140. London, National Gallery.* Signed and

Plate 72

FAMILY GROUP. Detail: the hands.

THE TRESCORE FRESCOES

(Plates 73–79)

The Chapel of Santa Barbara, adjoining the Suardi Castle at Trescore near Bergamo, is built "in the simplest form of church architecture, being a rectangle with a rafter ceiling and a shallow niche for the altar. Two windows and a door give light and ingress to the place" (Crowe and Cavalcaselle). In 1524, Count Battista Suardi gave Lotto the commission for decorating the portal wall, the two lateral walls and the ceiling of the chapel. This is borne out by an inscription recorded in full by Locatelli (1890). The frescoes were restored in 1941 by O. Della Rotta. (The length of the side walls is 8.12 meters.)

In this rustic setting, Lotto was to display his narrative mastery. Berenson is right in claiming that the creations here can only be compared on the one hand with Gothic, or on the other with Japanese works, and in stating that only in the *Intarsias* "his cursive narrative, his sense of beauty, his humor, his tenderness,

his power of giving the very vibration of movement, and catching the character of entire groups of people have had such free scope." Berenson shrewdly observes that a comparison with the pompous genre of Gentile Bellini and Carpaccio would be sufficient to show Lotto's amazingly modern achievement at Trescore.

FOLDED REPRODUCTION

THE LEGEND OF ST BARBARA. *Left wall, 812 × 456.* At the center a huge and bulkily painted Christ—at whose feet the donor and his family kneel in prayer—spreads out his arms and from the outstretched fingers of his hands vines branch out to the right and left and twine into frames along the top of the wall, each enclosing half-length figures of Saints: altogether, ten round frames enclose twenty Saints. At each end of the wall Giants, armed with billhooks are hurled down from the vine. They are the heretics Helvidius, Sabellanus, Paganus, etc., who want to destroy the mystic vine (plate 78). The rest of the wall depicts a charming vista of towers, houses, porticoes and *piazze* against a background of hills and woods. This is the scene in which the story of Barbara's martyrdom unfolds "as on Trajan's Column or the early Joshua Scroll" (Berenson), only broken in the center by the colossal Christ. The Saint appears, disappears and appears again; first we see her scorning the idols and fleeing from her idolatrous father who would kill her (plate 73); the chase continues—rather humorously—just above this scene, along a winding country track (plate 73, background); further right, Barbara is whipped with rods in the presence of a judge (plate 74, background) before being stripped of her clothes, hanged by the feet and beaten with mallets (plate 74); she is then taken to a prison where Christ appears and comforts her. After a second trial, the martyr is hanged by the hands and scorched with torches (see folded reproduction, scenes at the right of the central Christ). A new trial follows (plate 75) and the Saint, always preceded or followed by her faithful little dog, marches to her death in the midst of the awed populace—the women on the left (plate 76), the men on the right; children romp and tumble at the feet of the executioner and guards who are taking Barbara to her place of martyrdom (plate 77). The grim procession passes through the market place surrounded by red-roofed houses, an inn with a cardinal's hat over the door, the baskets of vegetables, apples and eggs laid out on the ground. Lotto could have made this legend into a veritable chamber of horrors, but the frescoes mitigate the cruel scenes so that they appear as so many incidents in a child's tale, even at the bitter end when the Saint is beheaded on the hill above the inn and a flash of lightning destroys her wicked father as her body is carried back to the village.

Plates 73–79

THE LEGEND OF ST BARBARA. Details: see above comment on the folded reproduction.

Plate 80

On the right wall, interrupted by a door and two windows, and under ten medallions with figures of Prophets and Sibyls, Lotto depicted scenes from the life of St Clare of Assisi. Each is vertically framed by pilasters.

ST CLARE TAKING HER VOWS. The Saint is lying face downwards on the altar steps while the Bishop, helped by his assistants, is officiating. Tremendous contrast is offered here between the cold white of linen and the creamier white of wool. On the right of the Crucifixion above the altar, St Clare is seen dispensing charity. A congregation of austere women at right, men at left and three restless children witness the ritual. In the medallions above we see David, the Erythraean Sibyl and Isaiah. (See also plates 81 and 86a and b.)

Plate 81

ST CLARE TAKING HER VOWS. Detail: women on the right.

Plate 82

MIRACLES OF ST CLARE. In the foreground, Clare is seen blessing the olive oil contained in two buckets; a short distance away a blind man leans on his stick; in the mid-distance the Saint saves a shepherd and his flock from a wild boar; at right, above the door, she is seen blessing the ripe crops and the reapers. In the medallions above are the Sibyl of Samos, the Prophet Jeremiah, and the Sibyl of Delphos.

Plate 83
MIRACLES OF ST CLARE. The Saint blessing the oil and taming the boar.

Plate 84
MIRACLES OF ST CLARE. Against a background of urban architecture rich with interesting detail, the Saint —left foreground—is depicted comforting the sick. She appears again at the loggia of the building seen at the right of the picture, as her prayers put the invading Saracens to flight. This scene has suffered from loss of color. In the medallions above are the Sibyl of Cumae, the Prophet Micah, and the Sibyl of Hellespont.

Plate 85a
THE BEHEADING OF ST CATHE-RINE OF ALEXANDRIA. *Portal wall.* The elegant executioner, seen from the rear, is about to inflict his deadly blow; soldiers and citizens surround the group; on the hills to the left a great fire destroys the philosophers whom Catherine has defeated.

Plate 85b
THE COMMUNION OF MARY MAGDALEN. *Portal wall.* Kneeling in the wilderness, the nude Saint worships the Host presented to her by a flying Angel. On the same wall are seven medallions with Prophets and Sibyls, all badly deteriorated.

Plate 86a
THE ERYTHRAEAN SIBYL. Detail: plate 80.

Plate 86b
THE PROPHET ISAIAH. Detail: plate 80.

Plate 87
CEILING. The pattern of grape vines originating from the hands of the Savior on the wall with the story of St Barbara continues among the rafters of the ceiling against a background of blue sky and Cherubs waving scrolls and bunches of grapes. This delightful fantasy is carried to the triangle above the portal wall.

THE INTARSIAS
OF SANTA MARIA MAGGIORE

(Plates 88–93)
Lorenzo Lotto drew and colored for the choir stalls in the Church of Santa Maria Maggiore at Bergamo thirty drawings of Biblical subjects as well as designing thirty-one allegories which were made into wood *intarsias* by G. F. Capoferri, G. Belli and others. Lotto worked on this enormous undertaking from 1525 to 1530. Documents relating to his payments show that he received the commission on March 12, 1524, after submitting two drawings in competition with other artists. His contract required him to provide pictures "*tam magnos quam parvos, pictos et coloritos*" (as many small ones as large, painted and colored) for the choir, at nine lire each, on condition that the drawings were returned to him once the *Intarsias* were finished. These drawings he treasured dearly, for in 1531 he claimed some of them back from a pupil to whom he had lent them, nor did he omit to mention them in his will of 1546: "the pictures of the Old Testament, which served as models for the *Intarsias* in the Choir at Bergamo;

and they are thirty pieces in all, that is twenty-six small ones and four large." The smaller paintings inlaid in wood can be seen on the choir stalls; the four "large" ones are on the choir screen facing the congregation. Besides the Biblical subjects, Lotto executed thirty-one drawings in chiaroscuro with allegories and "symbolic hieroglyphics." These were intended to become the cover-tablets for the stories, but in fact only four of them were used for that purpose; the remaining twenty-seven were inserted in the presbytery stalls of the Church. Apparently the master did not insist on the return of these drawings. The magnificent cycle of his *Intarsias* at Bergamo is unfortunately not so well known as it should be. In 1905, Berenson wrote: ". . . had Lotto been an engraver and scattered these designs throughout the world, instead of squandering them upon the church of a provincial town, it is likely that he would have come down to us as an acknowledged rival of Dürer." Later (1955), Berenson somewhat modified his praise.

Plates 88–89

THE FOUR PRINCIPLE INTARSIAS. *Panels, 70 × 103 each.* On the choir screen: *The Crossing of the Red Sea, The Flood, Judith and Holofernes,* and *David and Goliath.* As in *The Trescore Frescoos,* Lotto's narrative gifts find full expression in these scenes. Arcangeli (*Tarsie,* Tuminelli, Rome, 1943) expresses understandable surprise at how the bold translation from drawing to wood could have retained so much of the lyricism of Lotto's originals, and especially the inimitable relation between action and light.

Plates 90–91

THE SMALLER INTARSIAS. *Panels,*

44 × 46 each. On the back of the choir stalls. These are thirty *Intarsias* with Biblical subjects, but two of them (*The Annunciation* and *The Sacrifice of Abel*), on the two ends of the choir stalls, have slightly different measurements: *49 × 42.* The other subjects are: 1. *The Incest of Amnon;* 2. *Susannah and the Elders;* 3. *Moses and the Tablets of the Law;* 4. *Jonah and the Whale;* 5. *The Brazen Serpent;* 6. *The Death of Amnon;* 7. *The Refusal to Eat Pork;* 8. *Solomon and the Queen of Sheba;* 9. *The Vision of Elijah;* 10. *Joab Killing Amasa;* 11. *David Receiving News of Absalom's Death;* 12. *The Death of Absalom;* 13. *The Story of Achitopel;* 14. *David Cursed by Simei;* 15. *Samson and Delilah;* 16. *Samson with the Ass's Jawbone;* 17. *Samson and the Foxes;* 18. *The Parents of Samson Offering a Sacrifice;* 19. *The Selling of Joseph;* 20. *The Sacrifice of Isaac;* 21. *Lot and His Daughters;* 22. *The Sacrifice of Melchizedek;* 23. *The Drunkenness of Noah;* 24. *The Burnt Offering of Abel;* 25. *Creation of Eve;* 26. *Adam Teaches His Sons to Pray;* 27. *Creation of Man and the World;* 28. *Cain Slaying Abel.* Only *Intarsias* numbers 19 and 21–23 (plate 90) and numbers 11, 13–14, and 18 (plate 91) are reproduced here.

Plates 92–93

THE INTARSIAS WITH "SYMBOLIC HIEROGLYPHICS." *Panels, 60 × 50.* These are thirty-one symbolic inventions of such an extraordinary character as to put modern Surrealists to shame. Reproduced here are only eight examples of them, which are enough to give an idea of this aspect of Lotto's art. In 1955, Berenson wrote: "Of all attempts known to me as symbolism in art, these come nearest to being evocative without ceasing to be artistic."

53

LOCATION OF PAINTINGS

ALLENTOWN
(PENNSYLVANIA)
MUSEUM OF ART (S. H. Kress
Collection)
St Jerome Penitent (plate 32b).

ANCONA
PINACOTECA
The Assumption of the Virgin (plate
197).
SANTA MARIA DELLA PIAZZA
Madonna Enthroned with Four Saints
(plate 174).

ASOLO
PARISH CHURCH
The Assumption of the Virgin (plates
7–8).
Dead Christ in Landscape (plate
214; attribution).

BANBURY (OXFORD-
SHIRE)
UPTON HOUSE
Bust of a Dominican Monk (plate 18).

BERGAMO
ACCADEMIA CARRARA
The Martyrdom of St Stephen (plates
38, 41–42).
The Deposition (plate 39).
The Miracle of St Dominic (plate 40).
Portrait of Lucina Brembate (plate
53).
The Marriage of St Catherine (plates
64–66).
Holy Family with St Catherine
(plate 161).
Portrait of a Youth (plate 211;
attribution).

Sketches from the Legend of St Stephen
(plate 215; attribution).
CHURCH OF SAN BARTOLO-
MEO
Madonna Enthroned with Saints
(plates 36–37).
CHURCH OF SAN BERNAR-
DINO IN PIGNOLO
The San Bernardino Altarpiece
(plates 50–52).
CHURCH OF SAN MICHELE AL
POZZO BIANCO
God the Father Supported by Angels
(plate 98).
The Annunciation (plates 99a and b).
The Birth of the Virgin (plates 100,
102).
The Presentation in the Temple and
The Marriage of the Virgin (plate
101).
The Visitation (plate 103).
CHURCH OF SANT'ALESSANDRO
DELLA CROCE
Holy Trinity (plate 49a).
CHURCH OF SANT'ALESSANDRO
IN COLONNA
The Deposition (plate 47).
CHURCH OF SANTA MARIA
MAGGIORE
Intarsias (plates 88–93).
CHURCH OF SANTO SPIRITO
The Santo Spirito Altarpiece (plates
54–55).

BERLIN
STAATLICHES MUSEEN
Christ Taking Leave of His Mother
(plates 56–58).
Portrait of an Architect (plate 105).

55

Portrait of a Youth Against a Green Curtain (plate 106).
Bust of a Youth Against a Red Curtain (plate 114).
St Sebastian (plate 152a).
St Christopher (plate 152b).

LEPKE COLLECTION (formerly)
Double Portrait (plate 70).

BIRMINGHAM (ALABAMA)

MUSEUM OF ART (S. H. Kress Collection)
Portrait of a Man with Gloves (attribution).

BRESCIA

PINACOTECA TOSIO-MARTINENGO
The Adoration of the Shepherds (plates 129–130).

BUDAPEST

MUSEUM OF FINE ARTS
Angel with Globe and Scepter (plate 43a).
Apollo Asleep on Parnassus (plate 143).

CAMBRIDGE (MASSACHUSETTS)

FOGG ART MUSEUM
Portrait of a Dominican Friar as St Peter Martyr (plate 195).

CELANA (BERGAMO)

CHURCH OF SANTA MARIA ASSUNTA
The Assumption of the Virgin (plate 115).

CHICAGO (ILLINOIS)

J. W. ELLSWORTH COLLECTION (formerly)
Portrait of Christopher Columbus (plate 34b).

CINGOLI (MACERATA)

CHURCH OF SAN DOMENICO
The Madonna of the Rosary (plates 169–173).

CLEVELAND (OHIO)

MUSEUM OF ART
Man on a Terrace (plate 121).

COSTA DI MEZZATE (BERGAMO)

CAMOZZI COLLECTION
Madonna and Child with Two Saints (plate 61).

CREDARO (BERGAMO)

CHURCH OF SAN GIORGIO
God the Father (plate 94a).
St George Slaying the Dragon (plate 94b).
The Nativity with SS Rock and Sebastian (plate 95).
SS Jerome and Anthony of Padua (?) (plate 96a).
St Lawrence (plate 96b).
SS Bartholomew and Catherine of Alexandria (plate 97a).
St George (plate 97b).

DIJON

MUSEUM
Bust of a Woman (plate 6).

DRESDEN (formerly)

GEMÄLDEGALERIE
Madonna and Child with the Infant St John (plate 48b).

EDINBURGH

NATIONAL GALLERY OF SCOTLAND
Sacra Conversazione (plate 1b).

EL PASO (TEXAS)

MUSEUM OF ART (S. H. Kress Collection)

Portrait of a Man with Symbols (plate 185).

FLORENCE

BERENSON COLLECTION
Christ on the Cross with the Symbols of the Passion (plate 147).

CONTINI-BONACOSSI COLLECTION
Susannah and the Elders (plates 45–46).
Madonna and Child with Saints (plate 59).

R. LONGHI COLLECTION
St Peter Martyr (plate 43b).
A Dominican Saint (plate 43c).

PRIVATE COLLECTIONS
The Return of the Prodigal Son (plate 198).
The Entombment (plate 199).

UFFIZI
Portrait of a Youth (plate 2).
Virgin and Child with SS Anne, Joachim and Jerome (plate 162).

GIOVINAZZO (BARI)

CHURCH OF SAN DOMENICO
St Felix (plate 181).

HAMPTON COURT

ROYAL GALLERY
Portrait of Andrea Odoni (plates 123–24).

JESI

PINACOTECA
The Deposition (plate 28).
SS Francis and Clare (plate 107a).
Madonna Enthroned with Saints (plate 107b).
The Archangel Gabriel and *The Annunciate Virgin* (plates 108–09).
The Annunciation, lunette (plate 145a).

The Visitation (plates 145b, 146).
The St Lucy Altarpiece (plates 154–55).
Scenes from the Legend of St Lucy (plates 156–59).

KRAKOW (formerly)

PUSLOWSKI COLLECTION
Sacra Conversazione (plate 26b).

LENINGRAD

HERMITAGE
Christ Leading the Apostles to Mount Tabor (plate 30).
Virgin Nursing the Christ Child (plate 48a).

LONDON

BENSON COLLECTION (formerly)
Dead Christ Supported by Two Angels (plate 33a).

DUKE OF NORTHUMBERLAND COLLECTION
Cherub with a Skull (plate 49b).

NATIONAL GALLERY
Portrait of Agostino and Niccolo Della Torre (plate 35b).
Madonna and Child with Saints (plate 60).
Family Group (plates 71–72).
Portrait of a Lady as Lucretia (plate 136).

DOETSCH COLLECTION (formerly)
Portrait of Piero Soderini (plate 34a).

LORETO

PALAZZO APOSTOLICO
SS Rock, Christopher, and Sebastian (plate 153).
The Baptism of Christ (plate 201).
The Sacrifice of Melchizedek (plate 202).
The Recognition of the Holy Child (plate 203).
St Michael Driving Lucifer out of Heaven (plate 204).

The Adoration of the Magi (plate 205).
The Presentation in the Temple (plates 206–08).

MADRID

PRADO
Portrait of Messer Marsilio and His Bride (plate 69).
St Jerome in the Wilderness (plate 190).

MILAN

BRERA GALLERY
The Assumption of the Virgin (plate 31).
Portrait of Messer Febo da Brescia (plate 182).
Portrait of Laura da Pola (plate 183).
Portrait of an Old Man (plate 184).
Portrait of an Elderly Gentleman (plate 186).
Pietà (plate 189).

CASTELLO SFORZESCO
Portrait of a Young Man (plate 110).

CRESPI COLLECTION
Male Portrait (plate 144).

PRIVATE COLLECTIONS
The Toilet of Venus (plate 209).
Christ Leaving the Hall of Judgment (plate 216; attribution).

POLDI-PEZZOLI MUSEUM
Madonna and Child with Zacharias and St John the Baptist (plate 193).

MOGLIANO (MACERATA)

PARISH CHURCH
Madonna in Glory with Saints (plate 196).

MONTE SAN GIUSTO (MACERATA)

CHURCH OF SANTA MARIA IN TELUSIANO
The Crucifixion (plates 148–151).

MUNICH

ALTE PINAKOTHEK
The Marriage of St Catherine (plates 9a and b).

NAPLES

PINACOTECA NAZIONALE
Madonna and Child with Saints (plate 1a).
Portrait of Bishop Bernardo de' Rossi (plate 3).

NEW ORLEANS (LOUSIANA)

DELGADO MUSEUM OF ART (S. H. Kress Collection)
Portrait of a Gentleman (plate 160).

NEW YORK

HEARST COLLECTION (formerly)
Madonna in Landscape with Two Donors (plate 113).

NIVAAGAARD (COPENHAGEN)

HAGE COLLECTION
Portrait of a Man with a Rosary (plate 33b).

OSIMO

TOWN HALL (formerly)
The Recognition of the Holy Child (plate 168).

OXFORD

CHRIST CHURCH LIBRARY
Christ at Emmaus (plate 192).

PARIS

LOUVRE
St Jerome in the Wilderness (plate 10).
Christ and the Adulteress (plate 142).
The Recognition of the Holy Child (plate 163).

PHILADELPHIA

J. G. JOHNSON COLLECTION
Madonna and Child with Four Saints
(plate 44).
Portrait of the Surgeon Stuer with His Son (plate 188).

PONTERANICA (BERGAMO)

CHURCH OF SANTI VINCENZO
ED ALESSANDRO
The Ponteranica Polyptych (plates 116–19).

PRINCETON (NEW JERSEY)

UNIVERSITY MUSEUM
Holy Family with St Gabriel (plate 26a).

RALEIGH (NORTH CAROLINA)

MUSEUM OF ART (S. H. Kress Collection)
Martyrdom of St Alexander (plate 43d).
Dead Christ Supported by Angels (plate 43e).

RECANATI

PINACOTECA
The Recanati Polyptych (plates 19–23, 24a and b).
The Transfiguration (plate 29).

CHURCH OF SAN DOMENICO
St Vincent Ferrer in Glory (plate 27a).

CHURCH OF SANTA MARIA
SOPRA MERCANTI
St James the Pilgrim (plate 27b).
The Annunciation (plate 132).

ROME

CASTEL SANT'ANGELO
St Jerome in the Wilderness (plate 11).

BORGHESE GALLERY
Madonna and Child with Saints
(plate 17).
Portrait of a Gentleman Dressed in Black (plates 139–141).

DORIA GALLERY
Portrait of a Man Aged Thirty-Seven
(plate 166).
St Jerome in the Wilderness (plate 179).

GALLERIA NAZIONALE
The Marriage of St Catherine (plates 67–68).

PINACOTECA CAPITOLINA
Man with an Arquebus (plate 200).

ROSPIGLIOSI-PALLAVICINI
COLLECTION
The Allegory of Chastity (plates 137–38).

SANTA MONICA (CALIFORNIA)

PAUL J. GETTY COLLECTION
Portrait of a Jeweler (plate 35a).

SARASOTA (FLORIDA)

THE RINGLING MUSEUM OF
ART
Madonna with Sleeping Child (plate 165).

SEDRINA (BERGAMO)

PARISH CHURCH
Madonna in Glory with Saints (plate 180).

SIBIU (RUMANIA)

BRUCKENTHAL GALLERY
St Jerome in the Wilderness (plate 23a).

SIENA

PINACOTECA
The Nativity (plate 120).

SPLIT (YUGOSLAVIA)

MONASTERO DELLE PALUDI
Portrait of Bishop Tommaso Negri
(plate 122).

TRESCORE (BERGAMO)

SUARDI CHAPEL
The Legend of St Barbara (plates 73–79, folding reproduction).
St Clare Taking Her Vows (plates 80–81).
Miracles of St Clare (plates 82–84).
The Beheading of St Catherine of Alexandria (plate 85a).
The Communion of Mary Magdalen (plate 85b).
The Erythraean Sibyl (plate 86a).
The Prophet Isaiah (plate 86b).
Ceiling (plate 87).

TREVISO

PINACOTECA
Portrait of a Dominican Steward (plates 111–12).

CHURCH OF SAN NICCOLÒ
Heralds on the Onigo Monument (plates 212–13; attribution).

CHURCH OF SANTA CRISTINA AL TIVARONE
The Dead Saviour (Plate 12a).
The Santa Cristina Altarpiece (plates 12–15).

VENICE

CHURCH OF THE CARMINI
St Nicholas of Bari in Glory (plates 133–34).

CINI COLLECTION
Portrait of a Gentleman (plate 167).

PRIVATE COLLECTION
St Jerome in the Wilderness (plate 164b).

GALLERIE DELL'ACCADEMIA
Young Man in His Study (plates 126–28).

MUSEO CORRER
Madonna Nursing the Christ Child (plate 104).
Portrait of a Man Wearing a Red Cap (plate 210; attribution).

CHURCH OF SAN GIACOMO DELL'ORIO
Madonna Enthrone with Four Saints (plate 191).

BASILICA OF SAN MARCO
St Mark in Prayer (plate 194).

CHURCH OF SAN GIOVANNI E PAOLO
St Antoninus Altarpiece (plates 175–78).

VIENNA

KUNSTHISTORISCHES MUSEUM
Bust of a Youth Against a White Curtain (plate 16).
A Dominican Saint Preaching (plate 25).
Gentleman Holding a Golden Claw (plate 125).
Sacra Conversazione (plate 131).
Portrait of a Man in Three Positions (plate 135).
Christ in Glory with the Symbols of the Passion (plate 187).

WASHINGTON (DISTRICT OF COLUMBIA)

NATIONAL GALLERY OF ART
(S. H. Kress Collection)
Allegorical Scene (plate 4).
A Maiden's Dream (plate 5).
St Catherine of Alexandria (plate 62).
The Nativity (plate 63).

WILTON HOUSE (SALISBURY)

EARL OF PEMBROKE COLLECTION
St Anthony the Hermit (plate 164a).

SELECTED CRITICISM

Oh Lotto, as goodness good and as virtue virtuous: Titian from Augusta—in the midst of the great favors everyone is anxiously conferring on him—sends you greetings and embraces you in the letter that I received from him two days ago. . . .

Envy is not characteristic of you. Rather, you delight in seeing in other artists certain qualities that you do not find in your own work, although it none the less performs miracles which do not come easily to many who are quite content with their own technical skill. But holding second place in the art of painting is nothing compared with holding first place in the duties of religion. For heaven will reward you with glory that surpasses praise of this world.

PIETRO ARETINO
Letter, April 1548.

I believe he took advantage of being near Milan in order to study and imitate Leonardo in some things, though of course I would not believe history when it tells us that he was a pupil of Bellini and an emulator of Castelfranco [Giorgione]. . . .

These masterpieces and others in churches and picture galleries at Bergamo, make him a competitor of the great masters, and if he figures but little in Vasari, it is because that historian dealt only with less important works and with those that he [Lotto] had executed with less care.

LUIGI LANZI
Storia pittorica dell'Italia, 1789.

A most displeasing exponent of this [Bergamo] School is Lorenzo Lotto. His painting is so mannered that one finds it difficult to understand how, between 1510 and 1525, such a man could have been tolerated. He should have been stoned. I can hardly bring myself to repeat here what I observed in his work at Bergamo.

RUMHOR
Tre viaggi in Italia, 1832.

It is scarcely to be wondered at that the Venetian artist, in whom we first find the expression of the new feelings, should have been one who by wide travel had been brought in contact with the miseries of Italy in a way not possible for those who remained sheltered in Venice. Lorenzo Lotto, when he is most himself, does not paint the triumph of man over his environment, but in his altarpieces, and even more in his portraits, he shows us people in want of the consolations of religion, of sober thought, of friendship and affection. They look out from his canvases as if begging for sympathy.

BERNARD BERENSON
The Italian Painters of the Renaissance, 1959.

Even if modern art were not educating us as it is, to appreciate the technical merit of works like his, nevertheless, personality molding a work of art into a veritable semblance of itself is so rare a phenomenon in any age that we cannot afford to neglect it. Least of all should we pass it by, when that personality happens to be, as Lotto's was, of the type towards which Europe has moved during the last three centuries with such a rapidity that nowadays there probably are a hundred people like Lotto for one who resembled him in his own lifetime. His spirit is more like our own than is, perhaps, that of any other Italian painter of his time, and it has all the appeal and fascination of a kindred soul in another age.

BERNARD BERENSON
Lorenzo Lotto, 1895.

The principal attraction of Lotto at every period was brilliance and sparkling play of light; but those who closely study all his masterpieces will be struck by their inequality; they will find Lotto prone to fall into extremes, exaggerating contrasts of pattern and tint, exaggerating sprightliness and action, and forgetting the pure standard of taste in pompous dress and luxurious adornments.

CROWE AND CAVALCASELLE
A History of Painting in North Italy, 1912.

When one considers how many of Lotto's works went unacknow-
ledged or were attributed to other artists, one can say that no
other artist provides better evidence of the progress achieved
by art scholars in only half a century or more in establishing the
truth.

GUSTAVO FRIZZONI
in *Rassegna d'arte*, 1916.

The fact remains that Lotto's art, if compared with the epic and
noble manner of the painters of Venice, or if compared with the
"heroic majesty" of Titian, seems to be a vast naturalistic reper-
tory made up of humble particulars placed, sometimes whimsic-
ally and sometimes objectively, in a straightforward environment
of light and values. . . .

It should be clear that Lotto, far from searching for a form
previously molded by Renaissance conventions, adopted a sensitive, free and, above all, varied form in which beauty combines
with character. In brief, a constantly changing combination and
therefore a popular one in the finest sense of the word.

ROBERTO LONGHI
Quesiti caravaggeschi, 1929.

Lorenzo Lotto, with his blended, veiled tonalities, the quiet gray
atmosphere of his last period, his intimate good grace, left
Venice to found a great pictorial dynasty at Brescia and Bergamo,
and there to bless the marriage between Venice and Lombardy.
Those mobile atmospheres—especially in the predellas—which
seem to dissolve color and forms, have only one parallel in the
Italy of the Cinquecento, and that is in a few rare sketches by
Andrea del Sarto and in some of the impressions in the backgrounds of the great Annunziata frescoes.

ADOLFO VENTURI
Storia dell'arte italiana, IX, 4, 1929.

It is certainly because of Grünewald that Lotto broke up his neo-
Gothic colors into vibrations of light, and consequently almost
freed light from Renaissance concepts of spatial perspective. At

63

this point, Lotto's coloring reached an extraordinary qualitative intensity—as against Titian's conception of tonality. His counterpoints became increasingly adventurous, but the structural strength of his forms remained intact. In his research, Lotto reached the stage where he could devise effects of color reflected in light—and Veronese made good use of this.

RODOLFO PALLUCCHINI
La pittura veneziana del Cinquecento, 1944.

Lotto believes proportion does not exist. He believes that form, due to some inward restlessness, is constantly fluctuating, driven by some new "soul" that is involved with things beyond man. For Lotto, light is no longer a straightforward solar rule, a distributor of known and predictable effects, but a wandering, inconstant agent. Had his times understood the revolution implicit in his modest theories, Lotto would have assumed the role of "pastor to pictorial souls," and Venetian art (perhaps not only art) would have progressed toward Rembrandt rather than toward Tintoretto.

ROBERTO LONGHI
Viatico per cinque secoli di pittura veneziana, 1946.

It is still commonly accepted that Lotto's style was not consistent. This mistaken theory has been the reason why, when he was less well known, works of very different styles and quality were attributed to him. But there is perhaps no other technique that can reveal as constant a spiritual dedication as Lotto's, and this can be seen in each of his pictures. This feature alone should make him outstanding. He rarely lost his nerve when daring research led him along unknown paths, and yet he could also return with fervor and compassion to old roads that artists no longer followed. By now (the last period), he sensed that he had outlived his time and that shadow suited him better than full light. He had achieved rare freedom of expression, together with an ability to resume at random any motif required by mood and circumstance. In those times, at any rate, an artist could perfectly well be a craftsman and not lose face; and he could be Venetian in Venice, Lombard at Bergamo, Raphaelesque (or Mannerist) in the Marches. There was no shame in this: it was a sign of proficiency.

ANNA BANTI
Lorenzo Lotto, 1953.

But besides all these means of depicting the great divisions of light and shade within atmospheric masses, there was the question of relationship between light and objects and of their effect on one another. Objects—especially their surfaces—interested Lotto only in the sense that they reflected the movement of light. His world, as we have seen, is constantly seething: it is wrinkled, contorted, vibrating; as it strikes these angular surfaces, light splinters in many directions, but here and there, it catches and glows strongly. These flickering sparks express its fleeting movement, and are also the perfect symbols of the artist's own restless nature.

LUIGI COLETTI
Lorenzo Lotto, 1953.

Even in the nineteenth century Lotto must not have been greatly respected, for in 1861 Morelli and Cavalcaselle, requested by the Italian Government to evaluate Lotto's works in the Marches region, valued them no higher than those of Pagani or Sassoferrato.

PIETRO ZAMPETTI
in *Catalogo della mostra di Lorenzo Lotto*, 1953.

REPRODUCTIONS

ACKNOWLEDGEMENT
FOR PLATES

Fiorentini, Venice: plates 1A, 2, 3, 6–11, 16–24, 27A,
27B, 28, 31, 32B, 33B, 35A, 38–42, 45–47, 50, 51, 53,
55–59, 61, 64–68, 105, 106, 108, 110, 115–130, 132–
135, 137–141, 144, 145A, 146, 148–150, 154–162,
164B, 169, 174, 175, 177, 178, 180–184, 186, 191, 193,
195, 196, 206–211, 216; *A.F.I., Venice:* plates 12–15,
104, 107A, 107B, 109, 111, 112, 145B, 151, 170–173,
176, 212A, 212B, 213A, 213B; *Da Re, Bergamo:* plates
73–103; *Alinari, Florence:* plates 29, 48B, 52, 142, 153,
163, 179, 189, 202, 203; *Anderson, Rome:* plates 36,
37, 69, 166, 190, 204; *Gabinetto Fotografico Nazionale,
Rome:* plates 201, 205; *Perotti, Milan:* plates 54, 147;
Wolfrum, Vienna: plates 25, 131; *Studio dell'illus-
trazione, Milan:* plate 192; *Burnell, Sarasota:* plate 165;
plates 4, 5, 26A, 35B, 44, 60, 62, 63, 71, 72, 114, 136,
152A, 152B, 188, 197, 215A, 215B, 215C *are reproduced
by courtesy of the respective galleries.*

MADONNA AND CHILD WITH SAINTS
Naples, Pinacoteca Nazionale
(detail of plate 1a)

Plate I. MADONNA AND CHILD WITH SAINTS
Naples, Pinacoteca Nazionale
SACRA CONVERSAZIONE
Edinburgh, National Gallery of Scotland

Plate 2. PORTRAIT OF A YOUTH
Florence, Uffizi

Plate 3. PORTRAIT OF BISHOP BERNARDO DE'ROSSI
Naples, Pinacoteca Nazionale

Plate 4. ALLEGORICAL SCENE
Washington, D.C., National Gallery of Art

Plate 5. A MAIDEN'S DREAM
Washington, D.C., National Gallery of Art

Plate 6. BUST OF A WOMAN
Dijon, Museum

Plate 7. THE ASSUMPTION OF THE VIRGIN
Asolo, Parish Church

LAVRENTI LOTVS

Plate 8. *Detail of plate 7*

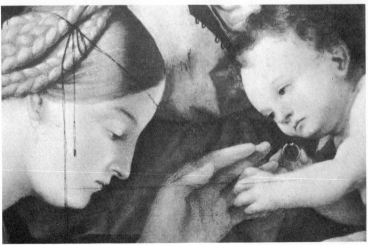

Plate 9. THE MARRIAGE OF ST CATHERINE
Munich, Alte Pinakothek, and detail

Plate 10. ST JEROME IN THE WILDERNESS
Paris, Louvre

Plate 11. ST JEROME IN THE WILDERNESS
Rome, Castel Sant'Angelo

Plate 12. THE DEAD SAVIOR and THE SANTA CHRISTINA
ALTARPIECE
Treviso, Parish Church of Santa Cristina al Tivarone

Plate 13. *Detail of plate 12*

Plate 14. *Detail of plate 12*

Plate 15. *Detail of plate 12*

Plate 16. BUST OF A YOUTH AGAINST A WHITE CURTAIN
Vienna, Kunsthistorisches Museum

PORTRAIT OF MESSER MARSILIO AND HIS BRIDE
Madrid, Prado
(detail of plate 69)

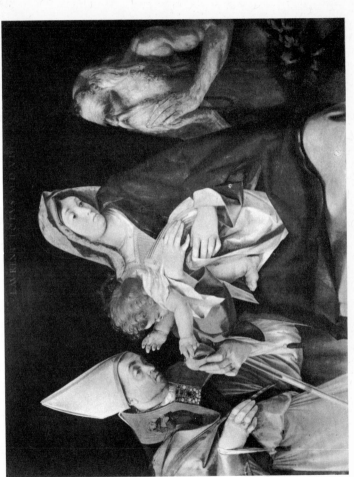

Plate 17. MADONNA AND CHILD WITH SAINTS
Rome, Borghese Gallery

Plate 18. BUST OF A DOMINICAN MONK
Banbury (Oxfordshire), Upton House

Plate 19. THE RECANATI POLYPTYCH: MADONNA ENTHRONED
WITH SAINTS
Recanati, Pinacoteca

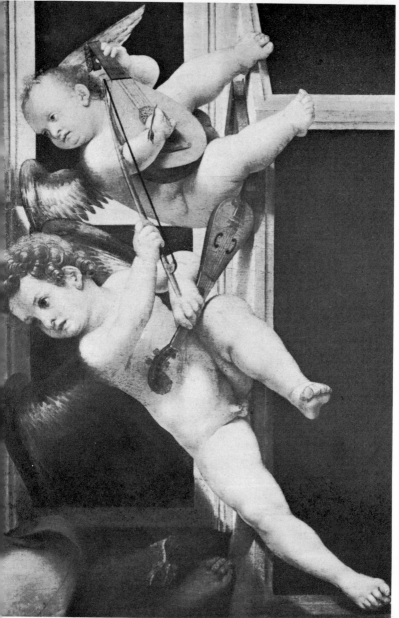

Plate 20. *Detail of plate 19*

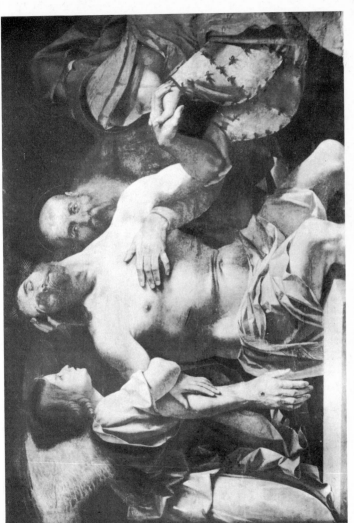

Plate 21. THE RECANATI POLYPTYCH: PIETÀ
Recanati, Pinacoteca

Plate 22. THE RECANATI POLYPTYCH: SS THOMAS AQUINAS AND
FLAVIAN
Recanati, Pinacoteca

Plate 23. THE RECANATI POLYPTYCH: SS PETER MARTYR AND VITUS
Recanati, Pinacoteca

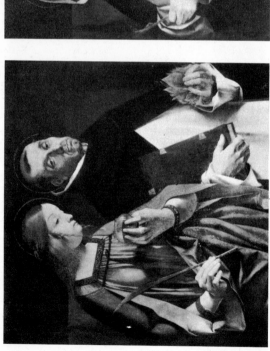

Plate 24. THE RECANATI POLYPTYCH: SS CATHERINE OF ALEXANDRIA
AND VINCENT FERRER and SS CATHERINE OF SIENA AND
SIGISMUND
Recanati, Pinacoteca

Plate 25. A DOMINICAN SAINT PREACHING
Vienna, Kunsthistorisches Museum

Plate 26. HOLY FAMILY WITH ST GABRIEL
New Jersey, Princeton University Museum

SACRA CONVERSAZIONE
formerly Krakow, Count Sigismund Puslowski Collection

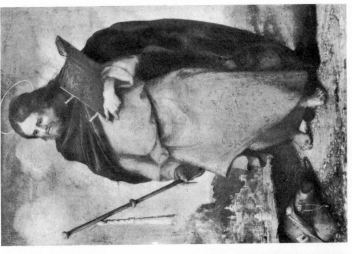

ST. JAMES THE PILGRIM
Recanati, Church of Santa Maria sopra Mercanti

Plate 27. ST VINCENT FERRER IN GLORY
Recanati, Church of San Domenico

Plate 28. THE DEPOSITION
Jesi, Pinacoteca

Plate 29. THE TRANSFIGURATION
Recanati, Pinacoteca

Plate 30. CHRIST LEADING THE APOSTLES TO MOUNT TABOR
Leningrad, Hermitage

Plate 31. THE ASSUMPTION OF THE VIRGIN
Milan, Brera Gallery

ST JEROME PENITENT
Allentown (Pennsylvania), Museum of Art

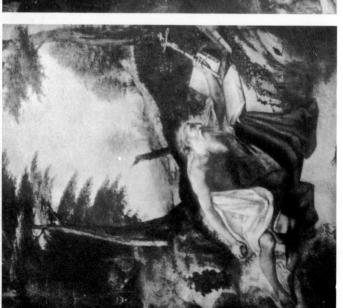

Plate 32. ST JEROME IN THE WILDERNESS
Sibiu (Rumania), Bruckenthal Gallery

THE LEGEND OF ST BARBARA
Trescore (Bergamo), Suardi Chapel
(*detail of folded reproduction*)

Plate 33. DEAD CHRIST SUPPORTED BY TWO ANGELS
formerly London, Benson Collection

PORTRAIT OF A MAN WITH A ROSARY
Nivaagaard (Copenhagen), Hage Collection

Plate 34. PORTRAIT OF PIERO SODERINI
formerly London, Doetsch Collection

PORTRAIT OF CHRISTOPHER COLUMBUS
formerly Chicago, J. W. Ellsworth Collection

Plate 35. PORTRAIT OF A JEWELER
Santa Monica (California), Paul J. Getty Collection

PORTRAIT OF AGOSTINO AND NICCOLÒ DELLA TORRE
London, National Gallery

Plate 36. MADONNA ENTHRONED WITH SAINTS
Bergamo, Church of San Bartolomeo

Plate 37. *Detail of plate 36*

Plate 38. THE MARTYRDOM OF ST STEPHEN
Bergamo, Accademia Carrara

Plate 39. THE DEPOSITION
Bergamo, Accademia Carrara

Plate 40. MIRACLE OF ST DOMINIC
Bergamo, Accademia Carrara

Plate 41. *Detail of plate 38*

Plate 42. *Detail of plate 38*

Plate 43. ANGEL WITH GLOBE AND SCEPTER, Budapest
ST PETER MARTYR and A DOMINICAN SAINT, Florence
MARTYRDOM OF ST ALEXANDER and DEAD CHRIST, North Carolina

Plate 44. MADONNA AND CHILD WITH FOUR SAINTS
Philadelphia, J. G. Johnson Collection

Plate 45. SUSANNAH AND THE ELDERS
Florence, Contini-Bonacossi Collection

Plate 46. *Detail of plate 45*

Plate 47. THE DEPOSITION
Bergamo, Church of Sant'Alessandro in Colonna

Plate 48. VIRGIN NURSING THE CHRIST CHILD
Leningrad, Hermitage

MADONNA AND CHILD WITH THE INFANT ST JOHN
formerly Dresden, Gemäldegalerie

THE LEGEND OF ST BARBARA
Trescore (Bergamo), Suardi Chapel
(*detail of folded reproduction*)

CHERUB WITH A SKULL
London, Duke of Northumberland Collection

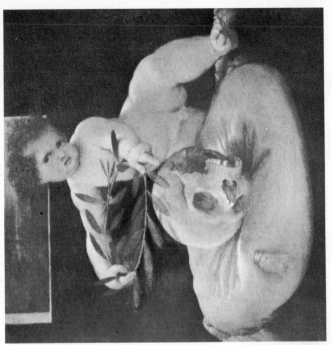

Plate 49. THE TRINITY
Bergamo, Church of Sant'Alessandro della Croce

Plate 50. THE SAN BERNARDINO ALTARPIECE
Bergamo, Church of San Bernardino in Pignolo

Plate 51. *Detail of plate 50*

Plate 52. *Detail of plate 50*

Plate 53. PORTRAIT OF LUCINA BREMBATE
Bergamo, Accademia Carrara

Plate 54. THE SANTO SPIRITO ALTARPIECE
Bergamo, Church of Santo Spirito

Plate 55. *Detail of plate 54*

Plate 56. CHRIST TAKING LEAVE OF HIS MOTHER
Berlin, Staatliches Museen

Plate 57. *Detail of plate 56*

Plate 58. *Detail of plate 56*

Plate 59. MADONNA AND CHILD WITH SAINTS
Florence, Contini-Bonacossi Collection

Plate 60. MADONNA AND CHILD WITH SAINTS
London, National Gallery

Plate 61. MADONNA AND CHILD WITH TWO SAINTS
Costa di Mezzate (Bergamo), Camozzi Collection

Plate 62. ST CATHERINE OF ALEXANDRIA
Washington, D.C., National Gallery of Art

Plate 63. THE NATIVITY
Washington, D.C., National Gallery of Art

Plate 64. THE MARRIAGE OF ST CATHERINE
Bergamo, Accademia Carrara

Plate 65. *Detail of plate 64*

Plate 66. *Detail of plate 64*

Plate 67. THE MARRIAGE OF ST CATHERINE
Rome, Galleria Nazionale

Plate 68. *Detail of plate 67*

Plate 69. PORTRAIT OF MESSER MARSILIO AND HIS BRIDE
Madrid, Prado

Plate 70. DOUBLE PORTRAIT
formerly Berlin, R. Lepke Collection

Plate 71. FAMILY GROUP
London, National Gallery

Plate 72. *Detail of plate 71*

Plate 73. *Detail of folded reproduction*

Plate 74. *Detail of folded reproduction*

Plate 75. *Detail of folded reproduction*

Plate 76. *Detail of folded reproduction*

Plate 77. *Detail of folded reproduction*

Plate 78. *Detail of folded reproduction*

Plate 79. *Detail of folded reproduction*

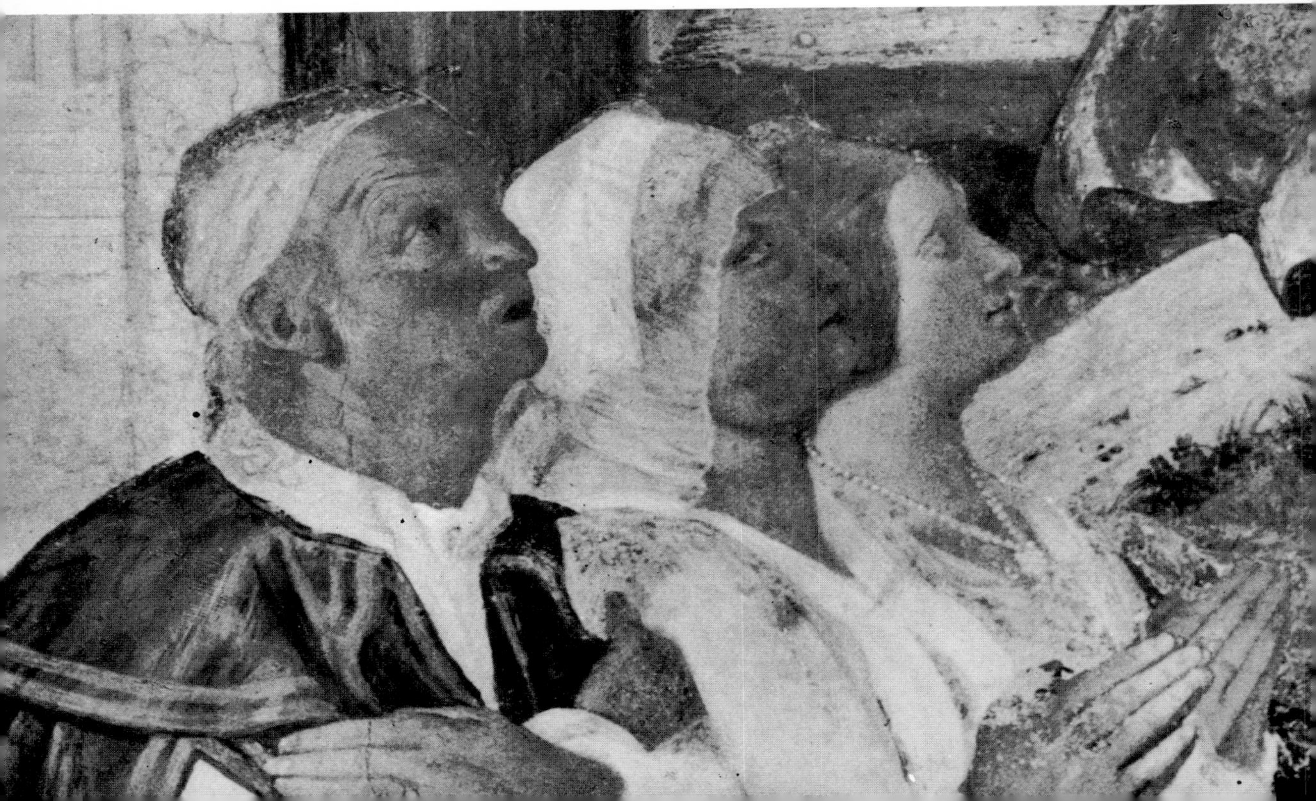

Plate 80. ST CLARE TAKING HER VOWS
Trescore (Bergamo), Suardi Chapel

Plate 81. *Detail of plate 80*

Plate 82. MIRACLES OF ST CLARE
Trescore (Bergamo), Suardi Chapel

Plate 83. *Detail of plate 82*

Plate 84. MIRACLES OF ST CLARE
Trescore (Bergamo), Suardi Chapel

Plate 85. THE BEHEADING OF ST CATHERINE OF ALEXANDRIA
and THE COMMUNION OF ST MARY MAGDALEN
Trescore (Bergamo), Suardi Chapel

Plate 86. THE ERYTHRAEAN SIBYL, and THE PROPHET ISAIAH
Trescore (Bergamo), Suardi Chapel

Plate 87. CEILING OF THE SUARDI CHAPEL
Trescore (Bergamo)

Plate 88. INTARSIAS
Bergamo, Church of Santa Maria Maggiore

Plate. 89. INTARSIAS
Bergamo, Church of Santa Maria Maggiore

Plate 90. INTARSIAS
Bergamo, Church of Santa Maria Maggiore

Plate 91. INTARSIAS
Bergamo, Church of Santa Maria Maggiore

Plate 92. INTARSIAS
Bergamo, Church of Santa Maria Maggiore

Plate 93. INTARSIAS
Bergamo, Church of Santa Maria Maggiore